Mystical Mushrooms

Mystical Mushrooms

DISCOVER THE MAGIC & FOLKLORE
OF FANTASTIC FUNGI

Aurora Kane

ROCK
POINT

First published in 2023 by Rock Point,
an imprint of The Quarto Group,
142 West 36th Street, 4th Floor,
New York, NY 10018, USA
T (212) 779-4972 • F (212) 779-6058
www.Quarto.com

Rock Point titles are also available at discount for
retail, wholesale, promotional, and bulk purchase. For
details, contact the Special Sales Manager by email
at specialsales@quarto.com or by mail at The Quarto
Group, Attn: Special Sales Manager, 100 Cummings
Center Suite 265D, Beverly, MA 01915 USA.

10 9 8 7 6 5 4 3 2 1

ISBN: 978-1-63106-921-5

Library of Congress Cataloging-in-Publication Data

Names: Kane, Aurora, author.
Title: Mystical mushrooms : discover the magic &
    folklore of fantastic fungi / Aurora Kane.
Other titles: Discover the magic & folklore of
    fantastic fungi
Description: New York, NY : Rock Point, 2023. |
    Includes bibliographical references and index. |
    Summary: "In Mystical Mushrooms, explore the
    magical properties, mythological connections,
    and symbolic qualities of ever-intriguing fungi"
    —Provided by publisher.
Identifiers: LCCN 2022042645 (print) | LCCN
    2022042646 (ebook) | ISBN 9781631069215
    (hardcover) | ISBN 9780760380048 (ebook)
Subjects: LCSH: Edible mushrooms—Popular works.
    | Mushrooms—Folklore. | Magic.
Classification: LCC QK617 .K287 2023 (print) |
    LCC QK617 (ebook) | DDC 579.6—dc23/
    eng/20221202
LC record available at https://lccn.loc.gov/2022042645
LC ebook record available at https://lccn.loc.gov/
    2022042646

Group Publisher: Rage Kindelsperger
Creative Director: Laura Drew
Senior Art Director: Marisa Kwek
Managing Editor: Cara Donaldson
Editor: Elizabeth You
Cover Design: Clare Skeats
Interior Design: Laura Shaw Design
Illustrations by Saga-Mariah Sandberg: pages 8, 12, 24,
50, 64, 80, 84, 86, 90, 94, 96, 98, 100, 102, 104, 106, 108,
110, 112, 114, 116, 118, 120, 122, 124, 126, 128, 130,
132, 134, 138, 140, 144, 146, 148, 150, 152, 154, 156,
158, 160, 162, 164, 166, 168, 170, 172, 174, 178, 180

Printed in China

For John,
in awe & honor
of the depth &
strength of the
threads of love
that bind us.

Contents

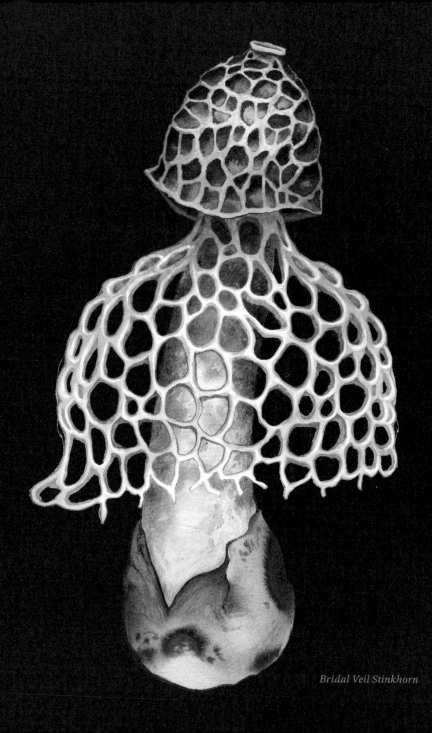

Bridal Veil Stinkhorn

Introduction

ZOMBIES, STINKHORNS, AND FAIRY RINGS—OH, MY! Welcome to the wildly fascinating world of mushrooms.

Mushrooms are at once mysterious, ominous, beautiful, feared, fascinating, edible, poisonous, mystical, magical, hallucinogenic, medicinal, virtually uncountable, weird, wild, disgusting, sometimes carnivorous, and at one time were even worshipped. Mushrooms are creation and regeneration. Mushrooms are the beginning, and mushrooms are the end.

Mushrooms are everywhere, seen and unseen, tricksters hiding in plain sight. In superstitious times past, their sudden appearance—and disappearance—seemingly out of nowhere and oftentimes in strange and fascinating shapes, even odors and colors, convinced many that evil lurked not far behind. Born of uneasy souls, lightning strikes, fallen stars, witches' work, gods, and the Devil, mushrooms were a force to be reckoned with.

Mushrooms have been known to us from the beginnings of human history but have existed far longer than we have known them. Researchers at the Swedish Royal Museum of Natural History found mycelial fossils in ancient lava flows in South Africa dating back 2.4 billion years: one billion years earlier than they were originally thought to exist, making them among the oldest-known inhabitants of Earth. Our earliest recorded references to mushrooms in the Western world come from the ancient Greeks and Romans discussing their edible qualities, and mushrooms have also been depicted throughout history in art, music, literature, poetry, and more. They symbolize luck, longevity, fertility and rebirth, prosperity, safety, change, resilience, learning, patience, and introspection, among many other beliefs.

Their long association with superstitions and witchcraft likely stems from their mysterious growth habits and seemingly spontaneous overnight appearance—especially as fairy rings—in strange, oftentimes human (phallic, fingers, and otherwise) shapes that carry malodorous stinks, as well as the hallucinogenic and poisonous properties of a small subset of mushrooms, and their quite bewitching ability to glow in the dark! Many common, or folk, mushroom names speak directly to their associated superstitions and the things they resemble: witches' cauldrons, Devil's fingers, elf cups, Devil's horn, Devil's tooth, witch's hat, death angel, dead man's fingers, and more. Their presence in fairy tales has nothing on the truth, which, in this case, may just be stranger than fiction!

Today, mushrooms are an epicure's delight. Historically, foraging for wild edibles, including mushrooms, has provided a free and easily accessible way to supplement one's food source, especially during times of famine, when the activity greatly increased due to practical needs. However, telling the edible from the poisonous has always been a conundrum, and not something to take lightly.

Their current and critical role in our ecosystems, recycling nutrients from dead or decaying organic matter and providing food and shelter for forest creatures—and, perhaps, even humans—cannot be discounted. As an industry, the edible mushroom market alone was worth a whopping $50 billion globally in 2021, with China as the leader in both cultivated and wild-harvested mushrooms. Research holds promise that the mysterious mushroom may bring medical cures and hope for many, as well as sustainable fabrics, fuels, and building materials, among their many other potential and futuristic uses.

Considering the magical, random nature of a mushroom appearing, when you see one, stop and count your blessings, for it is a sign of changing luck.

In our exploration of the marvels that are mushrooms, we will not look at their classification or identification—this is not a field guide and that is best left to the scientific experts—but rather at their more mysterious side, their magical, mystical qualities, history and lore, as well as the fantastical ways in which mushrooms are being used to enhance our daily lives. With an estimated eighty thousand known mushroom species, likely just a fraction of what actually exists (with the currently accepted potential number of all fungi on Earth being about two million), there is much to learn.

But we'll start small, with a variety sample of forty-three mushrooms, which will be covered in a little more detail. A few spells round out this discussion, if you're so inclined to work with their manifesting energies. And because mushrooms are of Nature, they offer a unique chance to explore, experience, and appreciate the wonders and benefits that Mother Nature provides. Some even believe that mushrooms represent the Moon's dark force within us, manifested in dreams and altered states of consciousness.

You don't have to go far in search of these wonders: a yard or park, a well-mulched garden or local forest, or a forgotten pile of decaying leaves can all be portals to this fantastic realm. Wherever you look, just being outside is a reason to slow the pace and absorb the calm, reconnect with our purpose, and renew our soul. Fall in love with the mystery that is mushrooms.

Honey Mushroom

The Fantastical Mushroom

ALL MUSHROOMS ARE FUNGI, BUT NOT ALL FUNGI ARE mushrooms! So, what *is* a mushroom?

The mysterious mushroom—even the origin of its name, "mushroom," is debated and as yet not *precisely* known—is the mainly above ground, fleshy, fruiting body of a fungus, usually comprising a stem attached to a cap, often umbrella-shaped, and often with gills. And although "fruit" implies "seeds," mushrooms instead develop microscopic spores rather than seeds underneath their caps or in tubes or sacs, which are spread by weather and animals. In proper conditions—wet and murky—these spores germinate into a sophisticated network of underground threads

The word "mushroom" likely derives from the French word *mousseron*, from *mousse*, meaning "moss," among which mushrooms are often found growing—though this is not a known certainty and is the subject of much debate. *Mushroom* first appeared in English during the mid-fifteenth century.

called the mycelium (or mycelia in the plural), which is basically the engine from which the mushrooms sprout. (And when the mycelia grow in a circle underground, they become the source of the infamous fairy ring; see page 137!)

A fresh mushroom is about 90 percent water (again, like humans), 5 percent carbohydrate, 3 percent protein, 1 percent mineral salts and vitamins, and less than 1 percent fat. Their scents range from being reminiscent of a rotting corpse (looking at you, stinkhorn, page 151) to sweet and enticing (hello, matsutake, page 173, and the lovely chanterelle, page 99). Their vast and varied uses range from nourishment to medicine, to decomposing plant waste and turning it into biofuel, to creating ethical and sustainable fabrics, to potential building materials for homes and other things.

And while a mushroom's life above ground can be fleeting, seemingly disappearing as fast as it appears, the mycelium from which it originates can feed off the Earth's nutrients and live for years—thousands in some cases and perhaps indefinitely—sprouting new mushroom crops when the time is ripe. In fact, two of the oldest, and largest, networks of *Armillaria* (not to mention two of the oldest and largest living things on Earth), include a relative of the honey mushroom (page 93) called the "humongous fungus," which was discovered by a small group of scientists in 1988 in

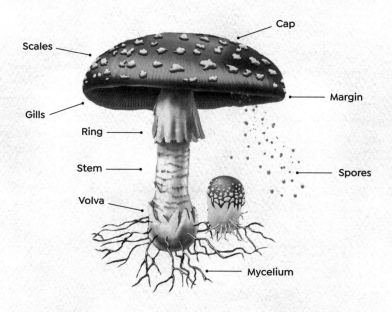

Cap
Scales
Margin
Gills
Ring
Stem
Spores
Volva
Mycelium

Michigan, publishing their first paper on it in 1992. Covering an impressive 37 acres (15 hectares), it is at least 1,500 years old and weighs at least 100 tons (9,700 kilograms). Ongoing research has determined that this particular monstrosity may actually be twice as large and almost twice as old as originally thought. And although this humongous fungus reigned supreme for a while, in 1998, another even bigger—"humongouser"—fungus was discovered. Malheur National Forest in Oregon now lays claim to the single biggest fungal organism: another species of *Armillaria,* one covering almost 3.5 square miles (9 square kilometers)—and spreading up to 3 feet (1 meter) per year—and that is almost 2,500 years old. And while these certainly get your attention for their sheer impressive size and age, mushrooms are also among the *smallest* living things on Earth.

In the earliest studies, which date back to the 1600s, mushrooms were thought to be an odd form of animal life. Later studies, moving into the eighteenth century, placed them with plants. Curiously, current

Research on mushrooms, in general, lags behind that of plants and animals in our understanding of this vast and varied kingdom. Because of the long and seriously held beliefs that fungi arose due to the Devil's handiwork, the Catholic Church did not approve of their study up until the nineteenth century!

research places mushrooms as more closely related to humans than plants in chemical makeup, even sharing similar DNA. And there's also a connection between mushrooms and humans that goes beyond the physical, one of spiritual and emotional energies. Not to mention the fact that they breathe in oxygen and breathe out carbon dioxide, just like humans. Deep breaths, everyone.

In recent years, interesting work on mushroom behavior and intelligence has revealed mushrooms' most amazing ability to adapt and respond to environmental conditions as evidenced in simplest form by the hyphae, the individual strands that comprise the mycelia, in their continuous and purposeful quest for food and nourishment. These mesmerizing discoveries fantastically demonstrate that fungi are capable of both learning and decision making, and they also possess short-term memory capacity.

Classification & Identification

Scientists generally believe that fungi led the way for plants and animals to exist on Earth. They were the first to leave water, separating from aquatic plant and animal life 1.5 billion years ago. As a transformative force of Nature, they helped create fertile soil, to set the stage for life on land. Plants "eventually" followed about 9 million years later, and survived, in part, by establishing their partnerships with fungi.

Today, mushrooms and all fungi—whose sheer numbers and variety are staggering and almost defy classification—enjoy status as a kingdom all their own, called fungi, which is separate from plants and animals and which can trace its ancestral roots back to a single organism. The difference comes in how they obtain their food. Fungi are further divided into classes, with two being:

* *Basidiomycetes*, spore-bearing mushrooms whose spores are exposed, and
* *Ascomycetes*, the largest class of fungi, comprising more than mushrooms, whose spores are contained in sacs

Just like a human fingerprint, key to a mushroom's identification is its spore print (see page 203). To obtain this, the mushroom's stem is removed and the cap is placed gill-side down on a transparent surface, such as a piece of plastic, overnight. As the spores are released from the cap, they create a powdery impression (just as when dusting for fingerprints!) that mimics the shape of the cap's gills (or pores, or spines, or so on).

Placing the transparent surface over either light-colored or dark-colored paper reveals the true colors of the spores. This impression is the spore print, whose most common colors include black, brown, cream, pink, purplish-brown, white (most common), and yellow. Other considerations for mushroom identification include whether juices appear upon breaking, bruising reactions, scent, taste, color, shape, habitat, and growing season.

A Mushroom's Diet

Like humans, mushrooms lack the chlorophyll that green plants possess, which means they cannot utilize sunshine to produce food and so must obtain it other ways. They do so by living in either parasitic or symbiotic relationships with other plants, or with dead and decaying matter. The mushroom's mycelium secretes digestive enzymes into the food source on or near where it grows. These enzymes break down the food source, and the mycelium absorbs these already-digested nutrients for nourishment (versus humans eating, then digesting their food internally, or plants creating energy from the Sun that nourishes their growth).

Although, in the absence of chlorophyll, mushrooms cannot and do not use light to produce their food or to grow (the mysterious mushroom can even thrive in the dark, making them *very* energy efficient!), some mushrooms do require small amounts of light for a few hours a day to fruit. And amazingly—and for mysterious reasons—some fungi contain up to eleven photoreceptors that sense the different wavelengths of light, which seems to affect their colors and shapes as they grow. Some mushrooms, like humans basking in the sunshine, even produce vitamin D when bathed in ultraviolet light. (Perhaps it even lifts their mood, too!)

Mushrooms—the ultimate recyclers—can eat just about anything, including plastic!

The Mushroom's Role

In their natural habitat, mushrooms not only provide food for the animals but also share nutrients with other plants and are a key player in keeping ecosystems balanced and healthy. They help decompose all manner of dead organic material in the woods, and elsewhere, that would otherwise pile up and overwhelm the environment. What they decompose, then, has a role in nourishing other plants, the soil, and the invertebrates that dwell there, to keep the cycle going.

Out of their natural environment, mushrooms are making equally amazing contributions to health care, environmental research and solutions, and varied industrial applications, including food and fashion, space research, architecture, packaging materials, biofuel, and many more. In short, they convert, support, and affirm life. With this portfolio of accomplishments, is it any wonder that mushrooms are considered wonderfully symbolic and capable of manifesting magic in whatever form they take?

Mushrooms send millions of tons of spores into the atmosphere every year, an amount significant enough to be a catalyst for clouds to form and develop raindrops. They can even conjure their own airflow to send those spores on their way to germination when none exists in the environment!

Mushrooms: Intelligent Life?

Instead of the search for alien intelligent life in our galaxy, some are beginning to think it lives among us in places previously unthought of.

Intelligence, or a higher consciousness, begins with simple sensitivity and awareness and becomes more sophisticated and complex with learning and memory. In current thinking, it is this basic sensitivity and awareness that is the level of intelligence being attributed to fungal life. Think simple communication or the passing along of information versus reasoned and critical analysis and interpretation of said information.

Research studies have shown that hyphae exhibit a simple memory to stress, for example, and can demonstrate adaptive behavior such as slowing growth rate and changing direction as a response—a kind of cellular consciousness. Also that the mycelia, which can be compared to neural pathways in the brain, have further "intelligence" regarding basic spatial recognition and memory in terms of growth location, and simple decision making demonstrated by how food is allocated through the mycelial network. Even basic problem solving can be counted among their skills, as they seek a growth path that delivers both nourishment and no obstructions to reaching their goal. These networks seem to grow and develop like a vast underground switchboard, connecting and relaying information where and when it is needed.

Their symbiotic relationships with trees and other host plants rely on sophisticated chemical interactions, or communication, if you will, that transmit information beneficial to all parties.

And although researchers are quick to note all the caveats in discussing fungal intelligence, just because we can't understand precisely what they're saying doesn't mean it isn't worth listening to the conversation or even learning the language so we can participate.

Mushroom or Toadstool?

The term "toadstool" in reference to mushrooms, particularly poisonous ones, exists in numerous languages and cultures across many centuries. Toadstools, too, it seems, were widely known for their hallucinogenic properties. The *Grete Herball* (1526), the first illustrated herbal directory in English, labels poisonous mushrooms as "tode stoles"—*tode* being German for "death."

As this distinction continued over many hundreds of years, the term "toadstools" was commonly used to distinguish edible mushrooms from poisonous varieties—the toadstools. And although a widely accepted principle, it was not necessarily an accurate one.

The belief that the slimy toad rested upon the toadstool's broad cap, imparting both his slime and poison to it, did nothing to help this cause. (Beware, too, lest the toad be a dwarf in disguise!) Not to mention the fact that both toadstools and tadpoles seemed to appear magically!

As knowledge of this vast, mysterious Fungi Kingdom has evolved, the term "mushroom" is now generally regarded as the (not necessarily scientific) one to describe those various fungi that produce the fruiting bodies, or mushrooms, we see above ground.

However, *tode* could also have been misinterpreted as "toad" of the amphibian kind, as many common toads were thought to be venomous—and associated with witchcraft—unlike frogs, and likely the reason there are no "frogstools." The British, historically, tended to call all mushrooms toadstools to indicate their disapproval of this vile entity, one certainly not fit for human consumption, and a cultural prejudice that seems to have trickled down through vast mycophobic cultures and generations.

Broadly speaking, other than that, mushrooms and toads have no known relationship outside of fairy tales, fairy kingdoms, and witches' cauldrons, leading to the conclusion that the concept of a toadstool as a resting place for a toad likely derives from folklore and superstition—and the odd witch's stew containing a pinch of both.

The toad's further association with witches, especially as familiars, and fairies is evident in many of mushrooms' common names, such as witches' cauldron (page 165) and fairy ink cap (page 105). One Central American tale explains that the sudden appearance of mushrooms after a rain is due to woodland spirits using the mushrooms as umbrellas throughout the night. As day breaks and the spirits retreat, they discard their umbrellas, which we then discover as toadstools.

A BAD REPUTATION DESERVED?

Mushrooms can be both hauntingly beautiful and repulsively disgusting. Their mysterious, seemingly magical, appearance and not always the prettiest presentation certainly contribute to their alien qualities—and what's unknown is often feared. Add to that the inherent difficulty in distinguishing with great certainty the edible from the deadly, and whether they must be cooked to be truly safe, mushrooms weren't always high up on the dinner menu rotation. Their long association with witchcraft didn't help. Despite being, basically, a free, local source of food (when not deadly), mushrooms have a decidedly divided fan base around the globe.

Nutritionally, edible mushrooms are loaded with vitamins, minerals, and essential amino acids. They're hormone-free, cholesterol-free, low-fat, and non-GMO, and contain anecdotal, proven, and yet-to-be discovered wide-ranging medicinal applications. They're versatile, delicious (some say), and easy to work with. So, what's the deal?

CAUTION!

Mushrooms should never be ingested when their source
is unknown and their identity is not 100 percent certain as
determined by an expert—then triple-checked.

Seems people are divided over mushrooms: some fear them, the
mycophobes, and some adore them, the *mycophiles*—terms coined by
R. Gordon Wasson, an American banker and mushroom enthusiast who
was famously inspired to study mushrooms during his honeymoon, in
1927, after noting the difference in attitude toward them between himself
and his new Russian bride.

Almost without exception, and for a long time, the Western world
lived in fear of mushrooms, whereas the Eastern world embraced
them. The French seem to have given them culinary legitimacy when
they incorporated them into their elegant cuisine somewhere into the
eighteenth century.

Mushrooms have always been alluring and mysterious. Today's
mushroom craze seems as though it popped up as instantaneously as
those mystical mushrooms that bring good luck and new opportunities,
but it's really, maybe, that we're just noticing something that's been there
all along, but in which we now see previously unimagined possibilities.

Liberty Cap

Mushroom Mystique

WHEN WE THINK OF FUNGI, WE TYPICALLY THINK OF mushrooms. However, the Fungi Kingdom includes not only mushrooms but also organisms like the yeasts that give rise to our breads, turn sugar into alcohol, and put the bubbles in our bubbly; and the molds that become the life-saving medicine penicillin and that distinctly flavor the cheeses we love so much. Their abilities to form beneficial (though, admittedly, sometimes destructive) relationships, as well as transform one thing into another, have led to fascinating discoveries, unusual ideas, and ingenious solutions to transform our world into a better place.

Here, we will look at some of the more bewitching, mysterious, mystical, magical, and intriguing aspects of fungal life. Get ready to be amazed.

Mushrooms & Witches

It's a stereotypical image: the elderly, often Eastern European woman, dressed in country garb and eagerly selling her carefully gathered mushroom treasures from a basket stacked high with her freshly foraged fare. The mushrooms gathered by these women became a source of knowledge and medicine for healing (and some hexing and charming), food for families, a way to earn money, and a conduit to community, as women often worked in groups to gather their mushrooms. Alternatively, being too successful too frequently in the hunt for mushrooms and applying their cures could get you branded a witch by town gossip and resented, even feared, by your neighbors.

Throughout history, women have been the keepers and gatherers of important and extensive herbal lore, including about mushrooms, and thus these natural healers, the "wise women," have become associated with mushrooms' properties to heal as well as harm. As part of an ancient culture, the wise women's role in society was traditionally valued and the women were routinely consulted for remedies and advice—even early physicians, herbalists, and scientists (men!) relied on the women's vast well of knowledge at the time.

The role of these wise women in their communities and the important contributions they made to them through their knowledge and actions cannot be overstated; yet they were simultaneously misunderstood, judged, and even persecuted. Women could not legally possess this knowledge, nor work with it in "true" professions whose ranks were held only by men; using this "illicit" knowledge could cost them dearly, for, in some countries and cultures, to use that knowledge to cure without the benefit of formal education was to risk being declared a witch and put to death as punishment. From 1500 to 1660, the number of suspected witches, mostly women, executed in Europe is estimated to be up to eighty thousand (Germany's deaths were highest, whereas Ireland had the fewest).

And, like the touch of a witch, it was a common belief that poisonous mushrooms turn silver spoons or silver coins black. Some documentation of other examples linking mushrooms and witches goes back as far as the sixteenth century—and even earlier—including:

* From the Spanish Inquisition, that witches used puffball mushrooms in potions.

* A Norwegian witch selling magical talismans, including mushrooms, to calm the seas.

* Malevolent witches turning food into toadstools.

* Mushrooms as charms, placed under the tongue to enhance the power of a kiss.

* Swedish witches crafting healing salves from mushrooms.

Witches were the frequent targets of blame when it came to crop failure of all kinds and the poisoning of livestock, along with the sprouting of those obscene fungi growing shamelessly in the garden. And those fungi were a frequent ingredient in any true witch's brew—along with the occasional toad. When seen growing in trees, the multi branching mushroom, *Exoascus* spp., or witch's broom, was a sure sign a witch had flown by on her broomstick, no doubt a warning to many.

THE TALE OF BABA YAGA

Mushrooms played a huge role in the diets of Russian and Slavic peoples, so it's no surprise to see them crop up in their folktales. The Russian tale of mushroom-hunting witch Baba Yaga, with a bit of a good witch/bad witch personality, was oft associated with the creatures and magic that dwelt beneath mushrooms growing on the forest floor. She was often pictured among the deceptively charming red fly agaric, which was definitely a tool of witches and from which some cultures believe the world was born.

Some scholars suggest that even her name, Baba (which can mean old woman, grandmother, or witch), may refer to a specific kind of mushroom, strengthening her relation to the fungi. An old folk song even tells us that mushrooms grow where old women go!

This crone, who dwells in the forest (really more of a swamp, where she guards the waters of life) in a hut supported by chicken legs (which was quite convenient, as the hut could be relocated on a whim), guarded the entrance from this world to the next, between humans and fairies, which some see as an agent of death and transformation. Perhaps in the same way mushrooms are agents of decay, or composting, and rebirth in new forms?

Baba Yaga was frequently seen riding through the air on her pestle, propelled by the mortar, and using a broom to sweep up any evidence of her flight. Whether benevolent or frightful, that depends on the tale. She may help you one day, take you prisoner the next, or eat you—oh, my! Legend says she was particularly fond of children for dinner. Her wretched appearance is quite frightening, but she has more of a trickster's soul than evil lurking there, using her powers to effect transformation.

FUNGUS & THE SALEM WITCH TRIALS

In seventeenth-century Puritan Salem, Massachusetts, witches and the Devil were "real."

What began in 1692 with some young girls playing a fortune-telling game and then subsequently experiencing unexplained convulsions, uncontrolled screaming, fever, and other unusual symptoms, led to the town's doctor diagnosing them as having been bewitched. As more and more townspeople exhibited similar symptoms, and claims of being possessed by the Devil grew, the village took up the cause (craze?) to root out and weed out all of the witches. The result of the hysteria (decidedly different than in earlier times of witchcraft accusations in Salem) was twenty-four people dead (nineteen hanged, one stoned, and four others who died awaiting trial) out of more than two hundred who were accused during the process.

One theory proposes that ergot poisoning is the likely explanation for the strange and unexplainable symptoms and characteristics exhibited not only by the accused "witches" caught up in the 1692 Salem Witch Trials, but by the participants and villagers as well.

The ergot fungus, *Claviceps purpurea*, while not technically a mushroom, is a member of the fungus family to which mushrooms belong. It grows on grains, commonly wheat and rye, and can be a cause of widespread crop devastation as well as a source of infection to humans who eat the tainted grains. It is highly poisonous and psychoactive, containing lysergic

acid, the active component of LSD. Ergot poisoning symptoms include delusions, hallucinations, vomiting, a creepy-crawly feeling on the skin, muscle spasms, seizures, and even gangrene of the limbs, fingers, toes, and nose. It was also known as St. Anthony's fire or the Devil's curse. Documentation dating to the Middle Ages details the deaths of tens of thousands from eating ergot-contaminated rye bread.

Delving deeply into court records and testimony of the trials, in 1976, Dr. Linnda Caporael came to the conclusion that the illnesses and symptoms described as a result of the "witches' curse" most likely were a result of ergot poisoning. The climate and weather conditions for its growth were ripe during the time and rye was a staple food crop, and the afflicted seemed to be concentrated in one specific area of town. By 1693, when supplies of the crop were running low, the craze ceased, as did the trials.

Of course, the evidence is not conclusive, and others attribute social, cultural, religious, political, psychological, other medical or poisonous factors, or a combination—even folk magic—as possible causes.

So, bad bread, witchery, hysteria, unknown illness, lies . . . maybe one day we'll know for sure. For now, it's a decidedly unlucky connection between "witches" and fungus.

Some theories put forth the idea that the fantastical beings, demons, and monsters portrayed in paintings by Northern Renaissance Dutch painter Hieronymus Bosch (c. 1450–1516) were inspired by symptoms of ergot poisoning, with his most famous fantastical depictions, perhaps, being displayed in his painting *The Garden of Earthly Delights*.

Fairy Tale Fodder

Fairy tales are universal. They're meant to entertain, certainly, but also to teach a lesson or social skill, and they were passed down in oral tradition before being written down in later times for posterity. Magic, mystery, witches, evil, and spells often help move the story along, making it, sometimes, a bit fearful but, more often, quite memorable. So, what's with all the mushrooms there, too?

Mushrooms pop up in fairy rings and in churchyards, they dot forest floors as resting places and dining tables, are in poisonous foods, serve as food for fairies, are used in magical potions, in deadly potions, and more. The association between mushrooms, toadstools, and fairies seems to have begun about the time that Shakespeare was writing, in the mid-sixteenth century, and it seems the strong belief in the connection between fairy rings, their mushroom components, and fairies helped spread the lore like mushroom spores! In Irish folklore, stone circles or monuments, oft believed to have been built overnight by fairies, sprung to life instantaneously in the same way that mushroom-populating fairy rings did.

OF FAIRY RINGS & BEASTS WITH WINGS

Where fairy rings are spied, it's said that elves, gnomes, and pixies do reside—evidence of festivity where dancing, song, and cheer abide. But beware, for strangers entering this realm oft never do return.

The seemingly supernatural fairy ring is the source of rich folklore and much speculation. Literally arising overnight, oftentimes under a Full Moon, what else could possibly explain the phenomenon of a magic circle of mushrooms appearing where none existed before?

If fairies there not be, then witches dance with glee—and one is wise to give them a wide berth. Tales from the French, German, and English tell of *ronds de sorcières* ("witches' circles" in French), where enormous toads with bulging eyes stood guard, and *hexenringe* ("witches' rings" in German), or hag's tracks in Sussex, England, formed by dancing witches celebrating the Full Moon, especially on Walpurgis night, the eve of Beltane: for much dancing takes place on May 1, May Day, as a celebration of fertility and the impending return of summer. Similarly, a Full Moon on Samhain, October 31, the witch's new year, is also a time of high revelry and when it's said that the veil between this world and the next is at its thinnest. The evidence of these celebrations lies in the perfect ring of mushrooms that has sprung forth along their dancing path, with the seemingly destroyed grass within. Even in early America, the lore of the dance within the fairy ring was strong: The Blackfoot believed the rings were caused by the dancing buffalo. More modern accounts say the rings mark UFO landing spots!

The Dutch claim the ring grows where the Devil churns his milk. Tyrolian folklore tells of winged dragons burning circles with their tails where toadstools then grow for seven years. British and Celtic tales recount fairies and elves dancing inside the ring, their feet so hot they burned impressions in the grass, with the mushrooms themselves serving as convenient places to rest when tired. Inside the ring, the elves and fairies do not like to be disturbed—so best to stay away lest you be forced to join the party and dance 'til the end of your days! But if you dare, dew collected there bestows luck in love and complexion fair!

And, in case you were contemplating this, destroying a fairy ring is not only terribly awful and very bad luck, it is also practically impossible. It will just grow back, only bigger and better than before.

Magic or science? Although believing in a glimpse into the magical fairy kingdom is more fun, science tells us that the fairy ring is always there, comprising the mycelium, the underground network that produces mushrooms, that grows in an ever-expanding ring in search of nutrients to feed its growth (which explains the dead grass and other decaying vegetation some rings leave in their wake). We really only take notice, though, when it sprouts the mushrooms it sends above ground. These rings, whether delight or nuisance, occur and reoccur naturally in forests, meadows, parks, fields, and lawns. One of the largest, found in France, is almost 2,000 feet (600 meters) wide and thought to be more than seven hundred years old. Another, almost one thousand years old, encircles the entire Stonehenge monument in England.

There are two types of fairy rings: *tethered*, which is usually spied in forests with a tree or two at its center as the mycelium is attached to the trees' roots from which it receives food in the form of sugar; and *free*, growing free of any specific source of food, usually in lawns and fields, where the mycelium feeds on dead or decaying matter found there. And of the vast number of mushroom species known, it is believed that hundreds are capable of producing fairy rings, with the most well-known being *Marasmius oreades* (page 137)—fairy ring mushroom or fairy ring champignon—native to North America and Europe. And remember, when you spy a fairy ring, not *all* believe it to be a place of darkness to fear; some believe it is a sign of fortune and good luck. In Russia and Switzerland, for instance, fairy rings mark the spot of buried treasure—but one that can only be retrieved with the cooperation of a witch or a fairy. So, stop for a moment and listen for the merriment below, then decide for yourself.

The Forest Aglow: Luminous Mushrooms

Though the stuff of fairy tales, this tale is true. Oft observed in cool woods and damp swamps at dark is a mysteriously ominous, greenish-blue glow. Is it a gathering of the forest fairies? A glimpse of the mischievous Will-o'-the-Wisp? The beckoning of a glow worm? The specter of a spirit? Known to woodsmen for ages, it is called foxfire, or sometimes fairy fire, and the observance of this phenomenon can be traced back as far as Aristotle, in the fourth century BCE, who called it a "cold fire" light.

The mysterious glow was one to be feared, marveled at, speculated on, studied, and used practically, such as to light one's path in the darkened forest or, as noted historically, to mark a soldier's helmet in the trenches of World War I to avoid colliding with fellow soldiers.

Though first written about by Aristotle (384–322 BCE) in *De Anima* as the phenomenon of "glowing wood," it was Francis Bacon (1561–1626) who was the first to study this phenomenon scientifically and prove conclusively that only dead wood glowed, and that it must be moist to continue to do so—the exact conditions required for fungi to thrive!

This ghostly glow is called bioluminescence, which is defined as the emission of light from living organisms, or the light so produced. The true source of this luminosity is from a reaction that occurs when the chemical luciferin reacts with oxygen, creating energy released as light, seen when certain species of fungi go about their business of breaking down and decaying wood. This is the same chemical that lets fireflies magically light summer nights and underwater beings twinkle like stardust.

However, it is not only the wood that glows. There are currently about seventy species of fungi identified as bioluminescent (mostly in tropical climates), or having the ability to glow in the dark. Examples include the jack-o'-lantern mushroom (Europe and North America; *Omphalotus illudens, O. olearius*; page 147), the ghost fungus (Australia and Asia; *O. nidiformis*; page 145), the moon-night mushroom of Japan (*O. japonicus*), and various species of honey mushrooms (Asia, Europe, and North America; *Armillaria* spp.; page 93).

Some mushroom species exhibit bioluminescence in all their parts; some only glow within their caps, and some only on their undersides. Other species emit a glow from their mycelial strands growing in soil or rotting organic materials, such as dead trees, rotten tree stumps, roots, and downed logs. In Northern Europe, when observed among leaf litter in fall, the source of the illumination is a charming bell-shaped toadstool, *Mycena tintinnabulum*. The glow is continuous, but only observed at night.

Why would they do this—are mushrooms afraid of the dark? One theory proposed it is a way for the fungi to release excess energy. Studies indicate that the fungi use the light to attract insect "pollinators" to them to help spread their spores, but this is only one possible explanation for the light show and the real purpose remains unknown.

Mushrooms Across Cultures & Religions

Our cultural and religious beliefs influence the way we interact with and interpret Nature, and mushrooms are a part of that. There are numerous beliefs regarding mushrooms and their influence on our lives—some modern, some ancient. A mushroom's common name is often a clue to some aspect of its relationship with people—whether feared, worshipped, or other. Here is a peek at enough information to give you a glimpse into the amazing widespread network that mushrooms have woven the world over.

To begin, know that finding a single mushroom is a sign of impending good luck and often also a sign of regeneration and rebirth, including pregnancy.

AFRICA

Among many African countries, mushrooms play a key role in culinary traditions and folk medicine. Their significance is highlighted in tales of their contributions to the creation of the world as well as extensive presence in folklore throughout the countries. In one such story attributed to the region of Central Africa, the Earth emerges from a mushroom, as from an egg, with the upper portion, as it splits, yielding the sky and the lower portion yielding the Earth. There then arose the mountains, stars, seas, rivers, Sun, plants, animals... all of life, and the Great Mother, Alonkok (the name of the mushroom itself).

In Yoruba culture, where the mushroom figures prominently, the mushroom *Termitomyces robustus*, a highly edible and nutritious food as well as one used for various medicinal applications, was a gift from the gods, and, alternately, dropped from the sky in the rain. It was associated with good luck and was used as a charm to conjure such luck. Annual offerings to said gods were a tradition to ensure a hearty mushroom crop.

In another Yoruba tale, a group of people fleeing danger saw mushrooms spring up in their wake, tricking the enemy into thinking they took another route, lest certainly they would have trampled the mushrooms, and thus saving those fleeing from an evil fate.

Nigerian traditions teach us the stinkhorn (pages 151 and 153) brings death and so it is said to make useful charms to protect against evil spells and enemies.

In some African beliefs, mushrooms are the souls of the dead.

ANCIENT EGYPT

Ancient Egyptians, like others, associated mushrooms with lightning, believing the mushrooms were heaven-sent as sons of the gods borne to Earth on lightning bolts. With such high status attached to them, mushrooms were only eaten by the pharaohs, who, in turn, believed that eating them granted immortality. (Unless, of course, that mushroom was poisonous, but that's a different story.)

ANCIENT GREECE & ROME

The ancient Greeks and Romans loved a good party, and that included a hearty feast, within which you'd find mushrooms held pride of place. And although some of the luxuries served at banquets were only within reach of those with the financial means to procure them, mushrooms were available to all, and great attention was paid to their proper preparation.

One of the earliest-known cookbooks thought to have been written in Rome during the first century CE, *Apicius: De Re Coquinaria*, contains numerous recipes for mushroom delicacies. Though not all agreed as to the contributions of fungi to the culinary scene back then, there was one thing that united them: the difficulty and importance of identifying edible from poisonous mushrooms. Roman author and naturalist Pliny the Elder offered his advice that any mushroom growing near rusty iron or rotten cloth would absorb its flavor and transform into poison, and, he added, as

In the superstitious Middle Ages, when magic was an everyday tool to be used to influence outcomes not always within one's control or understanding, mushrooms were deemed "magic." Without roots, flowers, or seeds, their seemingly unexplainable creation at will fascinated, and alchemists sought their secrets to creation.

would any mushrooms breathed upon by venomous serpents. (Alas, best be on guard during the season when serpents have not yet retired to their holes for the winter.)

This dilemma gave rise to any number of cautions and prescriptions: Avoid fungi that grow on yew and cypress trees; do not eat any fungi that blacken silver; garlic, a traditional evil repellent, will turn black when in contact with poisonous mushrooms; eat only fungi that can be peeled; beware the brightly colored fungi; if it doesn't soften after cooking, toss it; if it turns red after cooking, eat it; fungi harvested from the meadows are always safe to eat; cook them with meat or pears to neutralize their toxins; avoid the mushroom visited by serpents! Because none of these was accurate, they then also developed antidotes for when poisonings occurred (not always successfully, so better to be sure of what you're eating in the first place!).

Ancient Greeks believed mushrooms afforded great strength in battle, which, while anecdotal, is an idea that may have been rooted in real science. Mushrooms contain all nine essential amino acids the body needs to function properly and produce required amounts of protein, in conjunction with other foods, for strength and stamina.

Ancient Romans called mushrooms the food of the gods and one's social status at feasts and banquets was clearly communicated by the host, depending on the number and types of mushrooms served.

The association of mushrooms' origins and thunder and lightning is truly global. It is not just the ancient Egyptians; similar stories abound among Indians, Bedouins, the Chinese, French, Germans, Japanese, Māori, Persians, ancient Romans, and more!

First recorded by Aristotle in the fourth century BCE, the phenomenon of foxfire, the bioluminescent glow emitted by the honey mushroom (among other mushrooms; see page 33 for more) and that can be bright enough to read by, gave rise to the legend of Will-o'-the-Wisp. This elemental fiery fairy is well known in countries all over the world, appearing as a ghostly glow or flickering flame hovering above ground, rumored to lead travelers astray (variously into the fairy kingdom never to return, or to discover buried treasure!) and so was deemed either an omen of death or an illuminator of the path forward.

ASIA

A Daoist parable extols the mushroom as the principal food of the Eight Immortals, who have reached their exalted positions through an understanding of Nature's wisdom and secrets.

Ancient Chinese wisdom reveres mushrooms as the "spirit plant," believing they promoted longevity and bestowed spiritual wisdom.

Chinese culture past and present celebrates the shiitake mushroom for its aphrodisiac qualities as well as its related ability to restore vitality and virility.

In northern China, a traditional dish of stuffed black mushrooms, called *xiangu roubing*, meaning "a long and happy marriage," is a feature of many wedding feasts and banquets.

Called the Father of Chinese medicine, mythological Emperor Shen Nung, or Shennong (the Divine Husbandman), born in the twenty-eighth century BCE, created a catalog of 365 species of medicinal plants entitled *Shen-nung pen ts'ao ching* (*Divine Husbandman's Materia Medica*). Emperor Shen Nung included mushrooms by tasting and testing each one and dividing them into three categories: edible and medicinal; not-so-edible but with medicinal qualities; and poisonous. He gave this catalog to his people along with his knowledge of farming, and it is the source of China's expansive knowledge of medicinal plants and uses. Unfortunately, he died from a toxic overdose. Know what you're eating.

Japanese farmers say thunderstorms are good luck—they make the mushrooms grow! And centuries ago, Japanese nobility foraged for mushrooms in fall while elaborately dressed for the occasion and adhering to specific rules and customs.

The Leshy spirit guards the Russian forest and rules above all who live there. Wrinkles on mushrooms were attributed to the Leshy's whip, and he is known to be able to shrink small enough to hide behind even the tiniest mushroom in the forest. Beware this mischievous trickster and shape-shifter, able to change into even a mushroom.

Throughout Russian history, mushrooms were a mainstay of the cuisine owing to the great number of meatless fast days decreed by the Church. Additionally, Russian folk names for mushrooms often incorporate the tree on or by which it grows, demonstrating great knowledge of local fungi.

CANADA

The Indigenous Peoples living in what is now Canada have a few different beliefs about puffballs (page 135): Among the Haisla and Hanaksiala peoples, puffballs were thought to be harmful to your eyes, and if children went out alone into the night, ghosts would squeeze the puffballs into their eyes, rendering them blind. The Blackfoot believed puffballs were the transformed child of the Morning Star. The Secwépemc believed that when puffballs are thrown at you, you will become haunted by ghosts.

The Interior Salish, observing the strength of mushrooms to push through the ground and break wood and even asphalt as they grew, would bestow these traits of strength, intelligence, and independence on newborns by bathing the infants in the juice of mushrooms.

ENGLAND, SCOTLAND, WALES & IRELAND

Culturally, the English fear (and often despise) mushrooms. A common belief for those wishing to consume mushrooms was that they must be gathered only under a Full Moon to be safely edible.

The magically "insightful" fly agaric (page 87) happens to be in season during Samhain, which overlaps with Halloween, a time at which, it's believed, the veil is thinnest between this world and the next. Perhaps that explains the creatures of the night encountered frequently during this period. It's been told that fairy meet-ups were often on the agenda after a little fly agaric snack.

It's thought that the Druids prepared and consumed the fly agaric as part of their religious ceremonies in order to commune with the Universe and receive the great knowledge and enlightenment it could impart.

The Irish, in general, though typically wary of mushrooms, seemed to understand a lot about how mushrooms grow, recognizing their large underground web of connections and the fact that it could survive thousands of years growing there. As a result, the fruits of that web—the mushrooms—were eagerly sought for consumption so as to pass on the wisdom of the Earth they'd absorbed in their growth.

Remnants of stone circles and ancient dwellings found in Ireland are really ancient fairy forts.

The Gaelic word for mushrooms and fairies is the same: *pookies.*

The Welsh believe mushrooms are fairy food.

The eerie glow of the jack-o'-lantern mushroom was not a reassuring sight, but one believed to carry malicious intent, such as casting a spell with its glow, or leading you astray onto a dangerous path. The jack-o'-lantern's light was also believed to be the fiery creature of the marsh, Lantern Man, who could be unwittingly manifested by whistling. In such events, your only hope for salvation was to lie on the ground, face down, with your mouth buried in the mud!

Scottish folk were blessed with luck for a day when finding the bird's nest fungus (page 109) on the way to work.

In parts of England, gallitraps, or fairy rings, were the evidence of mischievous pixies stealing horses and then riding them wildly in circles in the fields.

EUROPE

In Eastern European traditions, especially in Poland, to be compared to a mushroom is a great compliment, as evidenced in the title of one particular folk song, "Our Bridegroom Is Like a Mushroom."

People of the Balkan countries placed dried mushrooms near windows or the hearth to protect their homes against witches.

In Slavic countries, where mushroom hunting is regarded as a national pastime, Christmas traditions frequently include a Christmas Eve mushroom soup—a tradition that was brought to the United States by European immigrants and still carried on today.

In Germany, at Christmastime, you'll find the iconic red-capped and white polka-dotted mushroom (fly agaric on page 87), called *glückspilz*, or "lucky mushroom," adorning all manner of Christmas decorations, including the tree, as a symbol of good luck and happiness in the New Year.

Owing to its earlier association with thunder and summer storms, a French proverb tells us that when rain pours down on St. Bartholomew's Day, there will be truffles aplenty.

A Croatian proverb wisely teaches that mushrooms are edible—but some only once.

In Sweden, witch's butter (page 171) was burned to ward off evil spirits.

A number of European countries share stories connecting Jesus, St. Peter, and mushrooms, including, for example, that while traveling together with little to eat, Jesus and St. Peter beg for food. Upon eating the bread they were given, both brown and white, crumbs from the white bread fall to the ground and sprout into edible mushrooms, whereas crumbs from the brown bread sprout poisonous toadstools.

In another, St. Peter is caught secretly consuming stolen cakes. Forced to spit them out, they become mushrooms.

MEXICO

Xochipilli, the Aztec god of flowers, is often depicted covered completely in entheogenic (see page 54), or divine, plants including sacred "magic" mushrooms (*Psilocybe mexicana*). Called *teonanácatl* in the native language, meaning "flesh of the gods", Xochipilli's face communicates the pure state of spiritual ecstasy derived from the use of these mushrooms.

Moctezuma's (also spelled Montezuma in English) lavish 1502 coronation as Ruler of the Aztecs brought with it a feast of *Psilocybe* mushrooms for the elite attendees. Apparently, much raucous fun was had by all, but a look into the future of Moctezuma's reign did not exactly turn out as well as predicted. Eventually, the conquering Spanish and Catholic missionaries outlawed magic mushrooms on penalty of death.

UNITED STATES

Sage wisdom from the Ozark Mountain people advises the best time to gather mushrooms is under a Full Moon (which others say also enhances their aphrodisiac qualities!).

An old Alabama tale, "Mushroom Toes," relates the story of the continued appearance of a group of ten mushrooms from a backyard grave. The source? The ten toes of the mistreated wife buried there.

In Hawaii, the mystifying Menehune ring, a.k.a. the infamous fairy ring, is credited to the Menehunes, a shy but slightly mischievous—yet highly skilled and industrious—Dwarf race inhabiting the mountain forests of the Hawaiian Islands since the beginning of time. They emerge at night to do their work—when they feel like it—but the Menehunes are not all work and no play: They love to make merry dancing and singing, with the result being... you guessed it, the Menehune ring.

The United States Department of Agriculture (USDA) reports that in the United States, 900 million pounds (408,000 metric tons) of mushrooms are produced each year and Kennett Square, Pennsylvania, the Mushroom Capital of the World, produces about 50 percent of those mushrooms.

Campbell Soup Company's popular cream of mushroom soup has been on grocery store shelves since 1934... that's a lot of green bean casserole (which followed in 1955) over the years! And, according to Campbell's, 50 percent of their cream of mushroom soup sales happen from November through January.

OTHER RANDOM BUT FASCINATING LORE

* When foraging, you're guaranteed abundant results while wearing at least one piece of clothing inside-out.

* Mushrooms were thought to be shy creatures, owing to the fact that they disappeared almost as quickly as they reappeared.

* Forget the mirror: kicking fungi will result in seven years' bad luck.

* The poor stinkhorn (pages 151 and 153) has been blamed for everything from cholera to insanity.

Mushrooms & the Arts

The arts reflect society and culture. They help us express our emotions, experiences, thoughts, beliefs, knowledge, and feelings as well as try to puzzle out our relationship with others and the world around us. The arts in all their forms are creative, reflective, communicative, thought-provoking, and tools for powerful social change. The arts are a record of history and of evolution. They help us connect and reconnect. They symbolize life emerging from the darkness.

In medieval art, mushrooms often depicted hell. Their murky origins, suspicious nature, and association with the Devil likely contributed to that. It didn't get much better during Renaissance times: Dung heaps and poison were the common denominator with mushrooms, but in 1675 the first book wholly about mushrooms, *Theatrum fungorum*, was published as an authoritative guide. The Victorian era, with its more modern aura of romanticism, established the connection between mushrooms, elves, and fairies, one that endures to this day. The psychedelic sixties spawned a mushroom culture that made the mushroom a celebrated symbol of freedom, bliss, and self-expression—in art and life. Today's culture of wellness and sustainability has forged a connection with mushrooms that links us at once to the past and to the future.

Some writers use mushrooms to symbolize destruction, evoke doom, or portend evil. Mushrooms in children's literature invite exploration, otherworldly adventures, and fantastical voyages. Others have invoked the mushroom to explore more sociocultural ideas. For example, "Mushrooms," a poem by Sylvia Plath, is a gentle evocation of a mushroom's growth and strength that serves as a metaphor for women's rights and evolution in society. Emily Dickinson's poem "The Mushroom Is the Elf of Plants," seems a wondrous examination of Nature, a frequent topic in her writing. In another poem entitled "Mushrooms," Paige Quiñones evokes the solitude of foraging within the larger concept of community and connection, represented by the mycelia network

In *The Tempest,* William Shakespeare references fairies "whose pastime is to make midnight mushrooms," reflecting the connection between fairies and mushrooms that was a popular belief during his time.

underground. This is but a spore in the large body of work that exists in poetry alone on the subject.

Mushrooms in literature are ripe for metaphors of death and decay, and can further a plot as murder weapon or feast, or indicate disapproval and evoke mood. Lewis Carroll likely includes one of the most famous mushrooms, the fly agaric, in *Alice's Adventures in Wonderland.* This is the presumed seat occupied by the hookah-smoking caterpillar whom Alice encounters once down the rabbit hole. Conversation ensues, whereby the caterpillar advises Alice about eating the mushroom: one side will make you grow smaller and the other side will make you grow larger—symbolizing many possibilities, not least of which is Alice coping with the changes that come from growing up. Even kids can get in on the mushroom fun: in *The Wonderful Flight to the Mushroom Planet* by Eleanor Cameron, two adventurous boys build their own rocket ship and fly it to the mushroom planet, Basidium (which is related to mushroom-producing fungi in real life!), where they find tree-size mushrooms growing wild and a population of little green men!

Mushroom depiction in all of the arts has been a "thing" since ancient times. And so prevalent are mushrooms in art that the North American Mycological Association maintains a Registry of Mushrooms in Works of Art (mostly Western paintings) tracking appearances and identification in works dating from 1300 to today's contemporary art, included from museum collections and exhibitions or those of established collectors, mentioned or depicted in a book or exhibition catalogs, or otherwise reliably known. The stated purpose of the registry is to "contribute to the understanding of the relationship between mushrooms and people as reflected in works of art from different historical periods, and to provide enjoyment."

MESMERIZING MUSHROOM MUSIC

"The Age of Aquarius" and the "Flower Power" movement are entwined with the psychedelic sixties, including the era's drugs, art, and music. Psychedelic chemicals, of which psilocybin, the chemical found in "magic mushrooms," is one, were touted for their mind-expanding effects when listening to music and the effects certainly spilled over into its composition. Contemporary studies have actually proven that psilocybin

increases the pleasurable experience and emotional response we have when listening to any type of music, not just that from the psychedelic sixties, by up to 60 percent, which also improves one's overall sense of well-being.

We have seen throughout history that Nature inspires artists, including musicians, to create brilliant compositions, but... can mushrooms actually make music? Some people say yes. Take Noah Kalos, a.k.a. MycoLyco, for one, who makes eerily seductive music by growing gourmet mushrooms and connecting them to synthesizers.

As all living things create electricity (energy), he sends that mushroom energy through a synthesizer in a process called biodata sonification to create sounds that at once suggest enthusiastic sophisticated underwater whale communication, surreal otherworldly techno vibes, atonal, sometimes almost tonal, melodies, video game interstellar galactic battle hymns, meditation, and joy—with different types of mushrooms producing different electrical frequencies and unique sounds, and even combining the energies from different mushrooms into magical duets. They must be, at least, part of the source of dance music heard in fairy rings, right? (Kalos is currently also experimenting with creating music with crystals... yes, please, how magical will that be?!)

Mushrooms also "spoke" to twentieth-century avant-garde and experimental American composer John Cage, an amateur mycologist who was co-founder of the New York Mycological Society. He has frequently been quoted as saying he could "hear the mushrooms in the woods." With Kalos's work, we can all now hear their melodious and alluring voices!

In an interesting parallel, and taking Nature's inspiration to new heights, acclaimed twentieth-century Czech composer Václav Hálek, who was also an amateur mushroom enthusiast, claimed that on one day around the year 1980 he could hear mushrooms singing in the forest—an entire choir and orchestra, no less. Once attuned to this phenomenon, his obsession "mushroomed" and he went on to combine his love of mushroom hunting with that of music, composing and transcribing

The Fungarium at London's Kew Gardens was founded in 1879 and contains specimens spanning the globe, from all seven continents. It is the largest (holding 1.25 million dried specimens), oldest, and most scientifically significant collection of fungi in the world and includes items collected by some of the world's most important scientists, including Charles Darwin.

thousands of melodies—from simple songs to full symphonies—inspired by what the mushrooms sang to him, each with its own melody to share. If you find yourself humming for no reason during your next walk in the woods, stop and look around you.

THE TALE OF BEATRIX POTTER & THE MYSTERIOUS MUSHROOMS

Our beloved Peter Rabbit may never have existed had Beatrix Potter's original fascination with Nature, specifically mushrooms and their study, been deemed a worthy career for women. About 350 original watercolors, which Potter painted beginning in 1887 when she was twenty, depict the varied mushrooms growing wild in the English Lake District where her family vacationed each summer. So keen was her interest in fungi that she obtained a microscope and successfully figured out how to propagate fungal spores—a topic about which little was known at the time, even in "scientific" communities. She used the microscope and her artistic talents to record their growth at various stages, as well as cross-sectional detail and images of spores, with her drawings and paintings illustrating things others did not even see! Both her interest in the subject and her observational skills were well developed.

With help from her uncle, the renowned chemist Sir Harry Roscoe, she made the acquaintance of Kew Garden's mycologist, who dismissed her work and her knowledge out of hand. In response, her uncle helped Potter prepare a paper for presentation, "On the Germination of the Spores of *Agaricineae*," at the Linnaean Society's annual meeting. As she was not a fellow (or member; the Society admitted its first female member in 1905), the paper was presented by another fellow of the Society, a man, as those were the rules at the time. No one seemed to care about her research, and it was noted that the paper needed more work. It was withdrawn and never resubmitted, so unfortunately, the paper was never published.

Speculation exists as to whether Beatrix's interest in mushrooms was more to fill a void than to pursue an actual occupation, and as to whether her work was as innovative and important as she thought or merely the reflection of an enthusiastic dabbler. Her paintings are lovely, and accurate, but her science may have needed more investigation.

Many of her mushroom drawings can be viewed at London's Victoria and Albert Museum as well as the Armitt Museum in Ambleside, UK, to which she bequeathed her many drawings, manuscripts, and other papers from her lifetime of work.

Werewere-Kōkako

Magical Shrooms

The "MAGIC" IN MAGICAL SHROOMS IS THE ENCHANTING, intoxicating, sometimes frightening otherworldly world these mushroom species create in us upon consumption. Freeing the conscious mind, stretching its limits beyond what we know, to experience life in new, exquisitely detailed and beautiful ways. Untethered by time, revealing secrets and past experiences and future civilizations and our place in the Universe, in meaningful context—twisting and changing, morphing and weeping— projected onto the mind's eye. Many who've had these experiences feel a deep spiritual component yet cannot adequately even describe them due to their power.

The cause of the magic is found in about two hundred different species of mushrooms, mainly within two groups: *Amanita*, to which the fly agaric (page 87) belongs and that contains the psychoactive ingredient muscimol, which is responsible for the mushroom's symptoms and effects, and *Psilocybe*, which contains the chemicals psilocybin (the most potent) and psilocin. The *Psilocybe* group is the one typically referred to as "magic mushrooms." Magic mushrooms are known to grow all over the world, in widely diverse climates and habitats, provided they receive enough rain. Two of the most famous in the group are the liberty cap (page 159) and the gold top (or gigglehead!), *Psilocybe cubensis*, the easiest of the two to cultivate.

All mushrooms within these groups, and the chemicals they contain, are classified as hallucinogens, psychedelics, and psychoactives. And although we know some of what these chemicals do to humans, what purpose they serve within the mushroom itself is still unknown and the subject of much speculation. Perhaps they serve as a defense mechanism? An adaptation and evolutionary strategy? Something else?

Early in our history, people discovered the medicinal and psychoactive properties found in the Fungi Kingdom. It may have been accidental or observational, but the connection was made between mushroom use and its ability to heal, ease pain, cause sleep, increase energy, and alter the mind in expansive ways. Mushrooms' use, then, was expanded beyond a source of food and fuel.

Fungi, most notably magic mushrooms, have been used and revered as sacramental tools to communicate with the spiritual world by many cultures for thousands of years. One theory, dubbed the "stoned ape" theory, however, put forth by ethnobotanist Terence McKenna and his brother, Dennis, in the 1970s, adopts the idea that psychoactive mushroom use is even more ancient than we think, and, perhaps, even a powerful influence on human evolution itself. They think a community of "proto-humans"—early hominids—would have eaten the mushrooms they found in the wild and then experienced psilocybin's profound effects on their brains, likening the reaction to that of software programming the brain, connecting and developing synapses, to enable the development of intelligence, cognition, and language, a reaction that eventually led to poetry, art, music, ritual, and more. Of course, this was not an instantaneous occurrence, but something that evolved over millions of years, and, importantly, hastened the evolutionary process, achieving a level of human intelligence far faster than if it had happened on its own. And though a number of primate species, twenty-three to be exact, including humans, are known to consume mushrooms as part of their diet, there is no definitive evidence to confirm, or deny, this theory. What do you think?

There are many examples throughout the Old and New World where "sacred" mushrooms appear as a central component of religious ceremonies. The oldest-known rock art (engravings and paintings)—a vast collections of some fifteen thousand pieces of art—depicting the use of psychoactive mushrooms comes from the rock shelters at the Tassili n'Ajjer Mountains UNESCO World Heritage Site, in remote southeastern Algeria on the southern edge of the Sahara Desert. The artworks date to the Neolithic period, when the desert would actually have been savanna with far more moisture in the environment, and include fearsome, mysterious-looking mushroom-clad shaman figures, thought to be shown wearing—even sprouting—*Psilocybe* mushrooms. Different interpretations exist.

India's Sanskrit texts refer to the legendary food of the gods known as *Soma*. Though not a universally accepted theory, the noted work of amateur mushroom expert R. Gordon Wasson concluded that the fly agaric (*Amanita muscaria*; page 87) is the original natural source of the mysterious Soma written of in the ancient text *Rig Veda* (c. 1500 BCE), where it's named as a favorite drink of the chief god, Indra, in his search for immortality. A Vedic Sanskrit word, "Soma" means "distill, extract, sprinkle."

Some historians think prehistoric cave paintings found in Spain and North Africa dating to 10,000 BCE may depict magic mushrooms.

Ancient Egyptian art depicts mushrooms and their various uses. Believed to have been buried directly into Earth by Osiris, this origin story earned psychoactive mushrooms the nickname "food of the gods."

It's fairly certain, too, that the ancient Aztecs revered the sacred mushrooms as the flesh of the gods, which they called *teonanácatl*, and consumed them in religious and spiritual rituals seeking wisdom from higher powers.

Even Plato and Socrates, in about the fifth century BCE, were thinking, and therefore philosophizing, about the spiritual qualities and brain-altering effects of certain mushrooms.

A collection of mushroom stone sculptures from Guatemala and nearby areas suggests that consuming psilocybin-containing mushrooms may have been part of ceremonial rituals dating back to the second millennium BCE. Ancient archeological sites here have been a rich source of mysterious mushroom stones since the eighteenth century. Nearly two hundred of these ancient stone statues, depicting gods or humans in the likeness of mushrooms and often incorporating mythic or real animals, have been found. Originally thought to be representative of some ancient mushroom cult, it is now believed these stones have significance to religious ceremonies in Maya culture incorporating hallucinogenic, or entheogenic, mushrooms, perhaps grinding them in preparation for consumption as well as in divination and spiritual work.

The first record of magic mushroom use in medical literature dates to 1799, in the *London Medical and Physical Journal*, and details the unwitting consumption of a meal of hallucinogenic mushrooms gathered along the River Thames, describing the effects on the youngest child in the family as (among other things) being stricken with fits of uncontrollable laughter.

Today, R. Gordon Wasson is credited with doing much of the research that unearthed what has become the basis for studying and understanding the cultural and religious contexts for the use of psychoactive fungi. His interest in the field of ethnomycology began during his honeymoon, when his new Russian bride discovered edible mushrooms on one of their walks in the Catskills. That discovery turned to a comparison of attitudes

Wasson promotes the term "entheogen," meaning "the God within us," as the respectful and properly descriptive term for the plant substances conveying the divine experience, instead of terms such as "hallucinogen" and "psychedelic", which (he said) trivializes their sacred place in cultural history.

between cultures about mushrooms, which eventually led to their studies in Mexico regarding mushroom use by the Indigenous Peoples of North America in religious ceremony. He claimed to have been the first Westerner to actually participate in the psilocybin ritual, in 1955, by which one communed with God to gain total enlightenment—and proving that the elusive practice was, indeed, still alive! Wasson's ensuing article on his findings, "Seeking the Magic Mushroom," published in *Life* magazine in 1957, not only gave us the first use of the term "magic mushroom" but also set off a cultural revolution of sorts.

So intriguing was the topic, even to the U. S. government, that the Central Intelligence Agency (CIA), under the assumed identity of the Geschickter Fund for Medical Research, secretly provided funding for his research trips to Mexico with the purpose of applying this new knowledge about hallucinogens to modern psychological warfare as part of its infamous super top-secret—and once discovered, highly troubling and controversial—Project MKUltra.

It was Swiss chemist Albert Hofmann, known as the father of LSD, who, in 1959, first isolated psilocybin. And the rest is, as they say, history.

Psilocybin (and other similar chemicals), the molecular component responsible for certain mushrooms' mind-altering properties, has a deep and often profound effect on human brains. Aside from its soul-searching,

Albert Hofmann was initially researching potential medical uses of ergot when he experimentally combined lysergic acid with diethylamine, which was abbreviated to LSD-25.

mind-bending properties, current and past research, as well as its history of Indigenous use for healing, indicates psilocybin may be helpful in treating severe depression by strengthening weakened connections in the brain that depression alters. (For some perspective on depression's place in our lives, the World Health Organization cites depression as the leading cause of disability around the globe.) Combined with music, the positive effect is even more noticeable. Psilocybin may also alleviate the stress and fear associated with terminal illness and death, among other real benefits to health.

The problem is, psilocybin, like heroin and ecstasy, is classified as a narcotic under the Schedule I list of narcotics, part of the United States' Controlled Substances Act of 1970, which means the U. S. government fears for its abuse and sees no current potential for accepted medical use.

During the 1950s and '60s, research on *Psilocybe* was common and cutting edge within the field of psychotherapy. However, psychedelic drug use germinated outside of the controlled lab setting, having been taken up by a youthful generation seeking to break free of societal constraint and make their own mark on the world, seeking their own magical mystery tour. The outcomes weren't all positive and as a result of the ensuing United States' war on drugs and psilocybin being outlawed in the 1970s, research on psilocybin's potential medical benefits became much more difficult to conduct. It should be noted, too, that other countries have made *Psilocybe* illegal and that its current status varies and is changing everywhere.

Things began to shift in the United States in the late 1990s as researchers, doctors, and others made the case for the potential medical benefits of *Psilocybe*. And recent breakthroughs, though small, are giving credence to psilocybin's possibilities and law makers are taking notice—and action, making it legal now for scientists and researchers to do their work. In the United States, cities such as Detroit, Denver, and Oakland decriminalized psychedelic mushrooms, and some states, such as Oregon, are following suit. As a result, in 2018 the FDA granted permission to the pharmaceutical company Compass Pathways to perform research with mushrooms as a treatment for depression, and in 2021, Johns Hopkins University received the first federal grant for psychedelic research treatment on psilocybin as a medicinal treatment for tobacco addiction, among other things, in fifty years. Additionally, Clerkenwell Health, based in London, will be conducting trials starting from August 2022 on using psilocybin to help people manage the anxiety that accompanies a terminal health diagnosis, the first study of its kind in the United Kingdom. As new information emerges and restrictive laws and views on psychedelic drugs change and relax, similar trials are ongoing and new research is set to begin in other countries, too, including Australia, Canada, Israel, and the Netherlands.

Designated so in 2015, September 20 has been marked as an "educational day of action" by noted mushroom activist Nicholas Reville, with the intention of fostering dialogue around the benefits of psilocybin.

CAUTION!

In the United States, psilocybin and psilocin are included in Schedule I of the Controlled Substances Act, and they're a Class A drug in the United Kingdom and elsewhere. It is, therefore, illegal to cultivate or possess psilocybin-producing mushrooms for personal consumption or distribution. Laws and restrictions may vary where you are.

JUST. SAY. NO.
Know your mushrooms. Consider your consciousness raised.

In the United States, psilocybin is currently being investigated as a treatment to help burned-out health-care workers processing grief and trauma from recent events, such as treating COVID patients. The active component of psilocybin improves the brain's connectivity and strips away the mind's control mechanism on emotions and just lets you feel them, which, it appears, can help alleviate the feelings of numbness and depression that many develop as coping mechanisms in extremely stressful circumstances. The study comes as a follow-up to previous studies that looked at psilocybin's ability to help cancer patients overcome depression and their fear of impending death.

The feather in this mushroom's cap, though, seems to be the wide range of therapeutic benefits it may be capable of providing, including saving lives, once its secrets are fully unlocked.

Food for Thought:
Meditate on This!

Psilocybin use is only one way to achieve spiritual harmony and open the mind to new experiences. Meditation, without the use of drugs, is another—and one that is widely used to reach a transcendent state on a par with what psilocybin can produce. Meditation has many similar consciousness-altering benefits to those that have been reported with psilocybin use. It has been said to contribute to overall improved physical and mental well-being, including helping develop a new perspective on stressful situations, reducing negative emotions and reactions, boosting creativity, fostering acceptance, decreasing pain, and increasing happiness. Research is currently underway exploring how the two, psilocybin and meditation, can work together to heal. For our purposes, though, we consider meditation the drug-free way to alter our consciousness and an important component in uncovering priorities and setting intentions for manifesting with mushrooms (see page 181), if you're so inclined.

MINDFUL MEDITATION

To meditate, in general, is to engage in contemplation or reflection, or a mental exercise (as when concentrating on your breathing or repeating a mantra) to reach a heightened level of spiritual awareness and to provide the unconscious room to work. Buddhists, who have been practicing meditation for millennia, believe it develops clarity, concentration, emotional positivity, and a calmness that is needed to see the truth. Meditation can also enhance overall well-being, which, in turn, can lead to increased self-confidence and understanding of our place in the Universe, an easing of depression, stress, and anxiety, and fostering a purposeful life or sense of fulfillment.

Mindful meditation is the practice of being present, where you strive for an increased awareness of being in the moment, *without judgment*, and paying attention to your body—your breathing, emotions, sensations, and thoughts that accompany or arise from it. Meditation is not about "tuning out" everything in our lives, but rather tuning in to the present—the good, the bad, the happy, the sad—and being gentle and accepting with ourselves.

Like psilocybin, regular meditation can bring about a transforming sense of relaxation and ease. Learning to focus your thoughts helps clear the clutter that can accumulate in our brains. It helps us see what's important and, more importantly, to just *be*.

Mindful Meditation Basics

Ready to give it a try? You don't need a lot of, or really any, fancy equipment or gear—only a quiet space (outdoors surrounded by Nature, such as on a quiet search for mushrooms, is a great option) and an open mind. Make this as fancy as you like, or as simple as just walking and breathing. Whatever you choose to do, make it regular and stress free.

* **FIND A QUIET, COMFORTABLE PLACE,** outside, if possible, to connect with the natural energies around you, ideal for boosting mood and peaceful feelings. Sit upright, lie down, or take a contemplative walk. Relax. Set a gentle alarm, if you want to time your session.

* **CLOSE YOUR EYES,** if you are comfortable doing so (of course, not if you chose a walk as your form of meditation), to limit visual distractions.

* **BREATHE.** Bring your attention to your breathing. Breathe naturally. Feel your body grow on the in-breath, and feel it collapse on the out-breath. Let yourself relax. Where do you feel your breath most?

* **IMAGINE** your inhale has the scent of roses or the earthiness of the forest, or as light, filling you from top to bottom, cleansing, clearing, and absorbing any negativity, hurt, or fear.

* **VISUALIZE** your exhale taking with it anything that's causing you pain, as you replace it on the inhale with soothing kindness.

* **FOCUS.** Keep your attention on your breath. When your mind wanders, gently acknowledge it and return your focus to your breath. Alternatively, as you continue your breathing, scan your body, focusing your attention solely on one part before moving on to the next—starting at your toes and moving upward to your scalp. If a particular part feels tense, uneasy, or painful, focus your mind and breathing on that part until it is relaxed before moving on. Again, if your attention wanders, gently refocus and continue the process.

* **BE GRATEFUL.** When your timer sounds, or you are ready, return your focus to your surroundings. Open your eyes. Wiggle your toes. Place your hands on the floor, in the dirt, on a tree, or on the chair in which you sit. Take a moment to give thanks for the quiet time and be grateful for the space that welcomes you before returning to your normal activities.

As with all new things we learn, mindful meditation takes practice and consistency. Even 10 minutes a day can help. Once you begin to feel the benefits in your life, you will crave the quiet peace that meditation affords.

As psychedelics and music combine for a total experience greater than its individual parts, research indicates that music, when combined with psilocybin to treat depression, amps up its positive effects. Studies have also shown that music improves meditation and its outcomes; whether it's the sound of the surf, your favorite jazz, new age, country, opera, or classic rock matters not. Music's vibrations affect our vibrations and can help clear emotional and physical blockages so positive energy once again flows freely.

While the "magic" in shrooms is chemical in the way it alters the mind's processes and, therefore, its consciousness, the "magic" in meditation is all within you. It is a powerful magic that opens space in your mind for your intuition to take hold and be heard, instead of the relentless chatter usually at play there, pushing everything else away. It is a magic of transformation—and acceptance. Of learning who you are, how you think, what you need, and what serves your highest purpose. It is the magic of gratitude that can, somehow, change your perspective on what's really important. It is a magic you can use to visualize that which you desire and direct to manifest your dreams. It is your magic. Use it liberally but heed it wisely as part of your best magical life.

Caesar's Mushroom

Mushroom Ingenuity

THE POWER OF MUSHROOMS TO SPEAK TO PEOPLE IN various ways, inspiring innovative uses and solutions, is nothing short of magical. Keen observation helps, as well as a genuine curiosity about the world and a desire to make a difference in people's lives and for the planet. Following are just a few amazing examples of how mushrooms contribute to the greater good.

The Case of Ötzi, the Iceman Mummy

One of the oldest examples of ingenious (and intuitive) mushroom use may be found with Ötzi, the 5,300-year-old "Iceman" discovered in 1991, entombed in ice on an alpine glacier in Italy's Ötztal Alps. (The evidence points to murder—the arrowhead in his back was a "dead" giveaway!) Among the items found with him were two different pieces of birch polypore, *Piptoporus betulinus* (now *Fomitopsis betulina*) carefully mounted on leather tassels and carried among his other equipment. Though these mushrooms are edible when young, Iceman did not have enough of a supply to be truly nourishing (plus they really don't taste great), leading to a conclusion that the mushrooms were used in a medicinal or spiritual way. They had a long association with Russian folk medicine, used to make soothing, immunity-enhancing teas as part of a cancer-curing regimen, and it is now proposed that Iceman may have used birch polypore as a means of ridding his intestines of parasites (of which he was definitely afflicted).

He also carried a pouch, kept safe from the elements, stuffed with "black matter," along with several sharpened flintstones in what looked like his fire-starting kit. Research determined that the black matter is the tinder fungus, *Fomes fomentarius*, whose primary use has been documented for innumerable centuries as tinder for fire-making, but that also has medicinal qualities, such as antibacterial, anti-inflammatory, antiviral properties, and the ability to help stop bleeding when used as a bandage.

Though Iceman lived to be only forty-six (his age estimated at the time of death) and he lived more than five thousand years ago, the evidence points to a sophisticated knowledge of local plant life—of mushrooms in particular, and their importance to survival and improving life.

Mushrooms in Medicine, Health & Wellness

From folk remedies to healing wounds, curing colds, or kindling romance to today's more scientific knowledge of the ability to boost immunity, treat diabetes, potentially cure cancer, and reverse the symptoms of brain diseases such as depression and Alzheimer's, the seemingly unlimited and as yet not fully understood role that mushrooms and their mystical properties can play in today's health and wellness is both enormously hopeful and admittedly mysterious. Let's consider just a few.

MUSHROOMS: NATURE'S MEDICINE

Traditional Chinese medicine has long revered the mushroom for its healing abilities—enoki, maitake, oyster, and shiitake are some of the most well known.

A long-held folk remedy in many cultures was to treat wounds with mold, a fungus like mushrooms, such as that found on bread (sometimes cloth, or leather, or other items, too), covering the wound with the bread like a bandage. Before penicillin was produced commercially from a mold during World War II, many soldiers' wounds were treated this way. Modern research tells us this was effective to a degree because the mold produced by the bread was actually a mild antibiotic.

Penicillin could, arguably, be one of the most important discoveries to date of a fungal by-product, and today we have many more: medicines that lower cholesterol, help prevent organ transplant rejection, treat severe infections, provide antiviral and anticancer treatments, ease depression and symptoms of Alzheimer's disease, and more. To learn how they work is as amazing as the cures they provide; if you remember from early chapters (see page 16), fungi are more closely related to humans than they are to plants. When we use medicines produced by fungi to solve their innate issues, curing disease, say, or as a defense mechanism such as killing pests competing for the mushroom's food, we react similarly to the compound because our molecular and biochemical makeups are so similar—and we reap their amazing benefits.

Historically, with mushrooms being classified as a plant, much of the knowledge and lore of healing with them was found within the herbal communities. Those who gathered, used, and kept the knowledge of curing with herbals were intimately familiar with the many local varieties and their varied uses, including which plants will heal and which plants will kill. Many of these folk cures were based on observation and have endured to inspire modern research.

In ongoing studies exploring the use of mushrooms and other fungi to develop sustainable packaging alternatives and New-Age building materials (see pages 74 and 75), other uses have been discovered. It's been shown that mycelium can be used to manufacture chitin, a main substance in mushrooms' cell walls, and that substance has been successfully used in clinical trials as a skin replacement to improve wound healing. We can only imagine the next amazing discovery now hidden within the mystery that is mushrooms.

The *International Journal of Medicinal Mushrooms*, published since 1999, aims to persuade health-care professionals to incorporate mushrooms into treatment protocols by publishing original research articles and critical reviews on a range of subjects pertaining to medicinal mushrooms.

CAN MUSHROOMS SAVE THE BEES?

In recent years, honeybees have been dying off in great numbers, significant enough to be of great concern not only for their future but also ours. This phenomenon, called colony collapse disorder, could likely be attributed to a number of things—pollution, insecticide use, habitat loss, and viruses are just a few. Because of a serendipitous observation made by mycologist Paul Stamets to bees being drawn to mushrooms in his garden, he began researching whether bees, *like humans*, could benefit from the many health benefits attributed to mushrooms. With researchers from Washington State University, he discovered that the bees did, indeed, benefit, perhaps from a boost in their immunity, and were able to fight off viruses linked to colony collapse. The bees were given an extract derived from both *Fomes fomentarius*, the tinder fungus, and the reishi mushroom. These two wood-rotting fungi are known sources of antiviral compounds with a long history of medicinal use for humans, especially in China. The link between Stamets's observations of the bees being drawn to mushrooms in his garden and the potential to use mushrooms' inherent healing properties was a genius hypothesis that proved true in its testing, and the experiments were deemed widely successful in improving the bees' ability to survive viral illnesses. Further research is needed, but the honeybees' future is already looking sweeter thanks to the magic of mushrooms.

MORE THAN JUST A PRETTY FACE

So, we know mushrooms are everywhere, but lately they're really *everywhere*—including in your skin care products. Though traditional Chinese medicine has recognized mushrooms' healing abilities, especially reishi—the mushroom of immortality—and Cordyceps, for just about everything for centuries, it seems that only recently have mushrooms come to the forefront of skin care, especially for those looking for a more holistic and natural approach.

Mushrooms, it seems, can use their innate powers to protect and heal our skin from external factors, like pollution and the stress of our busy lives, as well as fight internal stressors, like inflammation, to help it stay balanced and resist the signs of aging. Why the sudden surge? It seems popular culture and mushrooms' greater acceptance in our lives has us ready for such a seemingly unusual ingredient. It is no longer the pariah of the food world that it once was, and as people begin to learn and understand things about mushrooms that our ancestors knew long ago, these fungi are definitely having a moment in ways never dreamed of. Skin care is just one; with increased research and trials, and the public's demand for more natural, sustainable products, we learn more and more how mushrooms can affect our lives in significantly positive ways.

However, simply eating more mushrooms, or rubbing wild mushrooms onto your skin, will not produce the results you're looking for (so, don't do it!). As with all mushrooms, proper identification is key to harvesting their benefits (and avoiding accidental poisonings or other "irritations"), and that is best left to the professionals. But knowing which mushroom ingredients to look for as you forage for new products to buy and try can be helpful.

Mushrooms typically used in skin care products include the cauliflower mushroom, chaga, Cordyceps, jelly fungi, lion's mane, maitake, oyster mushroom, portobello, reishi, shiitake, tinder fungus, and turkey tail, among others. Products developed from mushrooms include those applied topically for their benefits, such as to firm, lift, smooth, brighten, moisturize, and reduce the appearance of wrinkles and levels of inflammation, as well as those taken internally as supplements in the form of pills, tinctures, and teas, to boost immunity and support beauty from the inside out. Those with topical applications, however, seem to deliver the best benefits directly to the skin.

So, even if you're not a fan of eating mushrooms, incorporating them into your skin care routine can be an easy way to take advantage of the many wellness benefits they offer.

The Mushrooming Food & Beverage Scene

The humble button mushroom and its kith and kin, long thought to contribute only taste or texture or some other "exotic" quality to meals, has risen through the ranks to superfood status—and beyond! Though there are still "lovers" and "haters" and the undeniable need to know edible from deadly, from pizza, risotto, a good stir-fry, spaghetti, and more, to farmers' markets, wild foraging, and grow-your-own kits, edible mushrooms are on everyone's radar today. And as an outgrowth of mushrooms' growing popularity, in general, and their health benefits specifically, "functional mushrooms," considered to be those with adaptogenic properties (meaning they help our bodies adapt to physical and mental stressors to help heal whatever ails you) and other recognized health benefits, are popping up in unexpected food and beverage places everywhere. Among the many who've noticed, Whole Foods and Kroger both named mushrooms as one of the top ten food trends in 2021—and one that wasn't going to stop there—and the *New York Times* called mushrooms 2022's Ingredient of the Year.

The global functional mushroom market, which includes food and beverages made from functional mushrooms, neutraceuticals, personal care products, and cosmetics, was worth almost $8 billion in 2022 and is expected to grow to about $20 billion by 2030.

Many of the mushrooms used for foods and beverages are the same as those you'll find in other health and wellness applications—chaga, Cordyceps, lion's mane, maitake, matsutake, oyster mushroom, reishi, shiitake, and turkey tail. And for many similar reasons: their anti-inflammatory and antioxidant properties, ability to improve circulation and boost immunity,

The beloved tomato ketchup was not always made with tomatoes. Originating in seventeenth-century China, the condiment was first a salty fermented fish sauce that also included nuts and mushrooms—highly reminiscent of soy sauce—and was used as a seasoning. In fact, the word "ketchup" derives from the Malaysian word *kĕchap*, meaning "fish sauce." In about the 1700s, it was adopted as an idea by English seafarers who encountered it in Indonesia and Malaysia, brought it home, and adapted their recipes for mushroom pickle into a sort of stewed mushroom paste-like sauce, adding a few "exotic" spices along the way. It was then that the concept of ketchup as a mushroom-based condiment (it must have been tasty, as it was known to be rather unpleasant to look at) became cemented. Early British Americans brought the tradition with them to North America, where it continued its evolution and "mushroomed" in both its popularity for use and variations based on local ingredients added to recipes. The growth of the tomato's popularity in later years added to the expanding repertoire of sauces known as ketchup, with the tomato variety today likely the one you think of when craving those fries.

positive effect on cognitive function, and benefits of easing stress, reducing anxiety, and increasing energy. They also bring vital vitamins and minerals to the table, as well as fiber and protein in low-fat, low-calorie packages. Some have proved even more beneficial to healing health problems like cancer and diabetes, as ongoing research reveals. Magic indeed.

We're far beyond your typical roasted, sautéed, grilled, stuffed, deep-fried, stir-fried, or cream of mushroom soup here. These mushrooms are being made into supplements, like pills, powders, tinctures, and teas, as well as beverages and foods that really pack the wellness punch and appeal to consumers' requests for healthy, sustainable, plant-based, beneficial products.

Mushrooms, especially their mycelium, and other fungi are being turned into sustainable, cruelty-free meat and dairy substitutes, called mycoprotein. Food products being made from mushrooms include bacon, "breakfast" patties, cream cheese, ice cream, "meatballs," "meat" crumbles, and burgers. Mushrooms are cropping up in seasoning blends and in

unexpected, packaged foods like mushroom jerky, crispy mushrooms as potato chip alternatives, Bliss bars, vinaigrettes, nut butters, and even sugar substitutes. Not to be left out, kombucha, juice drinks, and sodas boast functional mushroom ingredients and their benefits. Even coffee has joined the mushroom explosion. Touted as healthier than regular coffee and with less caffeine, yet carrying all the health benefits of the medicinal mushroom extracts they're made from, you can still enjoy your cuppa without all the typical side effects and boost your overall health and wellness at the same time.

And yes, mushroom cocktails are a thing. Get a bit adventurous on your next night out. Ask for a Truffle Pig or Truffle Old Fashioned, Mushroom Martini, Magic Mushroom, or Mushroom Manhattan. Perhaps I'm One Fungai or 'Shroom for Improvement sounds more your style. You might even find your cocktail served in a mushroom-shaped glass! Whatever you pick, mushroom cocktails are here to put "fun" into the party. Mushroom-infused spirits, like vodka, are also trending online and there are even some commercial options available so you don't have to make your own.

Myco-Architecture

Gnome homes and fairy flats on the Moon? As NASA continues to explore the world in which we live, away from Earth, practicalities are always a priority. Establishing new colonies on planets such as Mars, or on our Moon, means astronauts need basic necessities like housing, food, and water to do their work. One NASA project, the myco-architecture project, seeks to solve the problem of housing, without requiring the transport of heavy, expensive materials or ready-made structures for building, by growing structures from fungi mycelium. Known as synthetic biology, the field looks to find ways to utilize life itself as the technology. In this case, one way is growing habitable structures from fungi . . . basically,

Caesar's mushroom (page 85) was so prized in ancient Roman kitchens that it had its own vessel for preparing it, called a *boletaria*. Diners were given special amber knives with which to cut the mushrooms, as amber was not only more valuable than gold but also supposed to detect poisons.

with the end result being something you can water and watch grow! The tiny mycelial threads that create the mushroom fruiting body can be manipulated to create other structures (just as our bodies build bones, and skin, and organs) such as something similar to leather or plastic, or building blocks for a Mars astronaut condo—and furniture—all with its own ecosystem. Though sounding a bit science-fiction/fairy tale/fairy dust magic, this imaginative program has far-reaching benefits not only for space explorations but also for practical and sustainable applications on Earth for the benefit of humans (and maybe the random wee gentle folk passing through).

Mushroom Clothing & Accessories

Mushroom clothing these days is way more than funky prints and poufy skirts. Ecovative, a mycelium technology company, designs and grows sustainable materials originating directly from Nature, including food products, vegan leather, plant-based Styrofoam replacements, and other 100 percent-compostable packaging options designed for the beauty industry, intended to reduce the use and waste of plastics. And fabrics made from mycelium are not only sustainable, they're also hypoallergenic, naturally fire-resistant, nontoxic, and waterproof. A vegan mushroom leather handbag using Ecovative's innovative technologies licensed to a company called Bolt Threads and designed by Stella McCartney debuted on the runway as part of Paris Fashion Week 2022. Ms. McCartney is also currently exploring ways to use this technology to develop a replacement for animal-made silk fabric. And other big-name brands have also signed on to this option: Adidas and Hermès are just two more at the forefront of sustainable fashion.

Mushrooms & the Environment

Mycoremediation is the process of using mushrooms and other fungi to help repair the environment. As natural decomposers, they already help maintain a balance in ecosystems by converting and recycling dead plant and animal materials into usable nutrient-rich soil. They also absorb heavy metals and other contaminants from soil and water that can then be disposed of more easily, leaving in its wake a healthy place for humans, plants, and animals.

In a study including the United States Department of Defense, the turkey tail mushroom (page 169), an efficient composter, was one of only two found to be able to consume a potent neurotoxin (one used by Saddam Hussein in the Iran-Iraq War), as its primary source of nutrients, thereby neutralizing its threat.

Oyster mushrooms (page 155) are proving stars at oil spill cleanup, seemingly able to metabolize the oil, leaving the site clean and oil-free. And, spectacularly, oyster mushrooms have been trained to consume cigarette butts as a food source! Remarkable because most people don't realize cigarette butts—not straws—are the largest source of plastic waste in the world, currently 750,000 tons (680,389 metric tons) per year, and they contain hundreds of toxic chemicals besides.

Many of the projects currently being investigated are grassroots interests. Large-scale research and implementation are needed to make these, and more, a reality in our world, but the root change needed may just be found in the mycelium under our feet.

ALTERNATIVE FUELS

Just when we start to think mushrooms have given up all their mysterious secrets, another revelation comes along. This time, it's mushrooms' potential to develop sustainable biofuels as alternatives to fossil fuels. The ability to use mushrooms to produce biofuel is a more economical process, and one that could greatly reduce the amount of land devoted to growing crops, like corn, for biofuel and the amount of carbon released into the atmosphere along with it.

One seriously energizing by-product of the business of cultivating mushrooms is the discovery by a team of scientists at the National University of Singapore that the mushroom compost waste produced in the process contains bacteria that can convert cellulose (found in grasses, wastepaper, and wood) to biobutanol, a biofuel. Biobutanol is a liquid fuel that can replace gasoline, with no modifications, to power engines. And a researcher at the Swedish University of Agricultural Sciences has developed an even more efficient process for growing edible mushrooms and producing biofuel as part of a singular process. This streamlined process, which combines the separate steps of growing, harvesting the mushrooms, then collecting the cellulose, allows researchers to grow edible mushrooms, such as oyster and shiitake, on heat-treated wood, which cleans it of contaminants. As the mushrooms grow, they break down the wood, allowing the cellulose to be separated and then used to create biofuel. This simultaneous approach has increased yields and saves both time and money to create them.

The USDA's Agricultural Research Service has been investigating whether an enzyme in shiitake mushrooms that it uses to break down and dissolve the wood on which it grows can be souped up to digest other organic materials that could eventually lead to the production of ethanol.

And researchers at Stevens Institute of Technology, in New Jersey, are even discovering ways to use button mushrooms—that low-key variety from the grocery store—to produce electricity using a process they've dubbed "engineered symbiosis."

Serious fuel for serious thought.

Pink Waxcap

Mushroom Marvels

I T'S BELIEVED THERE ARE CURRENTLY FOURTEEN THOUSAND identified mushroom species, a mere drop (spore?) in the bucket of what it is suspected is yet to be discovered, which number about two thousand new specimens each year. And because we can't look at all mushrooms here, we'll start our journey into their mystical world with forty-three examples, selected to educate, intrigue, amuse, delight, and, sometimes, disgust.

BECAUSE WE'RE EXPLORING FACTS AND FEATURES *OTHER* THAN
TECHNICAL CLASSIFICATION, EACH PROFILE INCLUDES:

* An illustration

* The most common name and Latin name

* Comments about edibility

* Manifesting influence, for those who wish to explore mushrooms'
  magical side (beyond psilocybin)

* Other common names, as appropriate

* A description, with habitat, history, folklore, interesting features,
  medicinal applications (or other practical uses beyond culinary),
  color descriptors, and fun facts

NOTE: This information is intended to enlighten, entertain, and provide
food for thought. And while facts and illustrations are given with as
much accuracy as possible, this book is not intended as a field guide for
positive, authentic identification for any mushroom, nor does it advocate
any particular use, including ingesting it. That is best left to the certified
mushroom experts.

Don't think every mushroom is a jaunty cap set upon a sturdy
stem. You'll meet antlers, fingers, private parts, cups, cauldrons, caps,
cakes, chickens, nests, veils, tutus, zombies, deceivers, turkeys, truffles,
lions, puffballs, stars, teeth, undersea coral, and more—in all colors of
the rainbow.

Prepare yourself to get down and dirty with mushrooms in their
natural habitat and uncover some things you may not have known, wish
you didn't know, or may want to know more about.

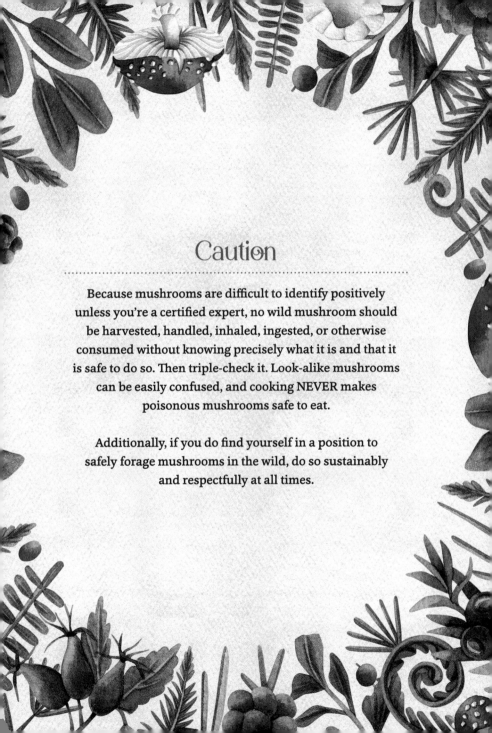

Caution

Because mushrooms are difficult to identify positively unless you're a certified expert, no wild mushroom should be harvested, handled, inhaled, ingested, or otherwise consumed without knowing precisely what it is and that it is safe to do so. Then triple-check it. Look-alike mushrooms can be easily confused, and cooking NEVER makes poisonous mushrooms safe to eat.

Additionally, if you do find yourself in a position to safely forage mushrooms in the wild, do so sustainably and respectfully at all times.

Amanita caesarea

Caesar's Mushroom

EDIBILITY ❖ Beloved; most highly prized at the egg (ovoli) stage, especially in Europe. Beware of other *Amanitas*, though, as many are extremely poisonous. Never ingest any mushroom unless you are absolutely, positively certain of what you are about to ingest.

MANIFESTING INFLUENCE ❖ Ambition, fertility, intuition, new beginnings.

OTHER COMMON NAMES ❖ Egg mushroom, ovoli mushroom.

COMMON ACROSS Southern Europe and into Northern Africa, this orange-capped mushroom is prized for its flavor, especially when harvested in the egg stage. And although Caesar's mushroom is one of the few edible species of *Amanita*, it's quite closely related to the hallucinogenic fly agaric (page 87), the deadly poisonous death cap (page 91), and destroying angel mushrooms. Take caution in your identification and respect the mushroom!

Said to have been reserved solely for the dining delight of the emperor, Caesar's mushroom is an Italian favorite and has been for more than two thousand years now, especially among the Roman rulers, nobility, and elite. One simple preparation for Caesar's mushroom that has survived these many thousands of years is to slice the mushroom raw (in its egg stage), then dress it lightly in olive oil, lemon juice, and salt. **NOTE:** Most mushrooms should not be eaten raw, so be sure you know what you're eating, and do not try this with other mushrooms.

The beautiful *Amanita caesarea* grows well near oak trees and sometimes pine. Its distribution outside of Italy, where it's frequently found along old Roman roads, is thought to be a result of Roman soldiers carrying the mushrooms with them as food. All hail, Caesar!

Amanita muscaria

Fly Agaric

❧≫≫⫷≪❧

EDIBILITY ⁖ Poisonous and hallucinogenic.

MANIFESTING INFLUENCE ⁖ Communicating with fairy beings and forest spirits, connecting with spirit guides, intuition, luck and abundance, protective spells and setting boundaries.

OTHER COMMON NAMES ⁖ Fly amanita.

THIS CHARMINGLY elegant, red-capped, polka dot–bespeckled, white-stalked mushroom is, perhaps, one of the most famous in the world—and straight out of a fairy tale. This forest dweller, common in most of the Northern Hemisphere, can grow up to 1 foot (30 centimeters) tall, and is definitely big and sturdy enough to support a wandering toad in need of a rest. Its red color is a symbol of passion and love and the charming white dots—some call them stars—speak of truth and clairvoyance.

Worldwide, the fly agaric serves as a magical symbol of an enchanted forest and its forest fairy and gnome dwellings; in German culture the fly agaric is even a symbol of good luck—like the four-leaf clover. There, it is called the Christmas mushroom and can be found on Christmas cards and decorations alike; it adorns children's books and exists cheerily and widely in pop culture—all belying its deadly nature.

Speaking of Christmas, did you ever wonder why Santa dresses in red and climbs down a chimney on Christmas Eve? Read on.

The fly agaric typically can be found growing under birches, pines, and spruce trees, which is, perhaps, our first clue regarding the fly agaric's association with Christmas, and sprouts between late summer and early winter. Coincidentally, this is also the time of year during which Samhain (Halloween) occurs; maybe not a coincidence at all, and an explanation for the myriad visions of fairies, witches, and spirits roaming the Earth on this night!

The fly agaric has a long history of both recreational and shamanic use in various cultures throughout Asia and Europe due to its hallucinogenic, spiritual, and healing properties. Aside from visions and intoxication, effects range from fearlessness, great strength, and stamina to states of joyous mania, hysteria, or deep sleep.

In central Asia, shamans dressed in ceremonial red garb—trimmed in white fur—and wearing black boots gathered the mushrooms for rituals. Returning to their huts with their foraged treats, or traveling onward to see clients to dole out medical or spiritual advice—or gifts on winter solstice—on their reindeer-powered sleds, they were said to enter the home through the smoke hole in the roof (because snow would be piled high against the door). After distributing the mushroom gifts, participants ate them and subsequently experienced euphoric visions of flying in vehicles pulled by horses, or reindeer, which apparently also become intoxicated when they've ingested this mushroom that they seem to favor as a food source. The fly agaric mushroom is also said to give a rosy glow to the complexion. Enter Santa, whose rosy-cheeked, red-suited self bears a strong resemblance to the shamans themselves, or the fantastical mushroom. Common winter solstice rituals included stringing dried mushrooms to decorate the hearth, much like we do today with dried fruits, popcorn, and pine boughs.

In northeastern Siberia, where this mushroom was historically gathered to serve as provision for the harsh winter months, it's said that those too poor to barter or trade for it would brave the weather, waiting with bowls outside dwellings to collect the urine of mushroom-imbibing Siberians, which they then drank up (cheers!) and from which they derived the same effect as by consuming the mushrooms themselves!

The Druids used the fly agaric ceremonially to gain great knowledge and enlightenment and to communicate with the Universe. Irish lore acknowledges the great depth and breadth of knowledge contained within the underground network (mycelium) of fungi, which it received from the ancient Earth, and believed consuming mushrooms, sprouting from this knowledge, was a way to absorb its wisdom. In Austria, the mushroom was known as *hexenpils*, or "witches' mushroom."

Though not a universally accepted theory, the noted work of R. G. Wasson concludes that the fly agaric is the original natural source of the mysterious Soma, the ritualistic drink of the Hindus, written of in the ancient text *Rig Veda*, where it's named a favorite drink of the chief god, Indra, in his search for immortality.

And, though frequently depicted as its iconic red-capped self, the fly agaric exists in a range of colors, including shades of yellow, orange, and scarlet. Its name, "fly agaric," derives from its recorded use to kill flies, the first of which was by the German writer Albertus Magnus dating to the thirteenth century CE. (It doesn't actually kill the flies, but it does disorient them long enough to be swatted.) Some argue that the name refers to the fantasy of flight experienced under its effects.

NOTE: In your search for immortality, it is highly advised that you do not consume the toxic cocktail that is the fly agaric, though if you are lucky enough to find one, using it in a spell or two, symbolically (see page 181 for ideas) to manifest your dreams is allowed.

Amanita phalloides

Death Cap

EDIBILITY ❖ Deadly poisonous.

MANIFESTING INFLUENCE ❖ Endings, truth.

OTHER COMMON NAMES ❖ Death cap, destroying angel
(also an *Amanita* variety, but a different mushroom).

WITH A NAME like death cap, this must be the work of the Devil! A transplant from Europe—its most infamous, no less—the death cap is one mushroom capable of sprouting fairy rings, and its deadly nature may be just one reason fairy rings are as feared as they are. That, and the fact that it's a trusted ingredient in a witch's hexing powder among those who practice black magic. A rumored murder weapon and killer of emperor and king, even Agatha Christie would be impressed by the deadly poison found lurking here. The mushroom emerges from an egglike membrane in late summer to late fall, typically growing in woods or their edges and often found among the oaks. It can grow up to 6 inches (15 centimeters) across.

Just a single mushroom of this deathly white, sometimes shiny or metallic looking when dry, yet unassuming-looking species will definitely make you sick: deadly sick. Just ask Roman emperor Claudius (10 BCE–54 CE), who died a frightful death after ingesting a meal of mushrooms served up by his fourth wife, Agrippina, who "allegedly" substituted a plateful of death caps for his favorite Caesar's mushroom, *Amanita caesarea* (page 85). (Why murder him and not just divorce him, you ask? She was making room for her son, Nero, from another marriage, whom Claudius had adopted, to inherit the throne.) This notorious mushroom is also credited with killing a king, Charles VI of Austria, head of the House of Hapsburg, which led to the War of Austrian Succession (1740–1748) and morphed into a global conflict.

As demonstrated by Claudius, who did not notice the substitution, this deadly mushroom is often mistaken for similar-looking mushrooms that are edible, like the false death cap, and its typically white-gilled, greenish-yellow cap can appear in a number of colors, making true ID that much more confusing. It's said that one cap contains enough poison to kill eight people! Worse, the mushroom's poisonous effects are delayed, not appearing until twelve hours or more after ingestion, contributing to a difficult diagnosis if you are affected, and by then it has shut down the liver and kidneys. This single mushroom accounts for nearly 90 percent of deaths caused by mushroom poisoning. Just say no.

If your intent is to use this for manifesting, remember to do no harm, to yourself or anyone else. Seek inspiration in its coloring, which can speak of Earth and grounding, common sense, renewal, truth, and manifesting thoughts.

Armillaria mellea

Honey Mushroom

EDIBILITY ⁘ Its culinary attributes, though debated, are typically deemed unimpressive—and they can make you sick. As well, it can be confused with other inedible species and, so, best to avoid ingesting it at all.

MANIFESTING INFLUENCE ⁘ Balanced emotions, illumination, rooting out deception, steady growth.

OTHER COMMON NAMES ⁘ Honey fungus.

D**ON'T LET** the sweet name and fair-faced appearance of this mushroom fool you. It's not nearly as sweet-natured as it sounds.

Once thought to be a singular type of mushroom, the honey mushroom actually comprises a dozen or so biologically discrete species found the world over that look very much alike, with *Armillaria mellea* among the most well known. This parasitic mushroom is often found growing in honey-hued clusters at the roots of trees or in stumps. Finding them in your yard or garden could also signal trouble. It attacks the root system of certain shrubs and trees and can be hugely destructive as a result of it spreading through the soil by way of shoelace-like structures until it connects with other plants and trees as its network continues to expand and destruct—for miles.

Its color suggests personal power and self-esteem and its growth habit certainly supports this energy.

The honey mushroom does have some sweet statistics to its name, though. Because of its vigorous mycelial growth habit, the honey mushroom can actually survive and grow for *thousands* of years, with sufficient food and appropriate climate, spawning massive numbers of individual colonies. This capability means the honey mushroom now holds the record not only for the largest living organism we know, but,

perhaps, also the oldest. A colony of honey fungus in Oregon discovered in 1998, estimated to be 2,500 years old, now claims the title of world's largest (in area), covering nearly 3½ square miles (9 square kilometers)—and spreading up to 3 feet (1 meter) per year. And though the first-discovered honey mushroom "humongous fungus," identified in Michigan in 1988, seems to pale at only 37 acres (15 hectares) and 1,500 years of age, it still does hold the record for largest in weight (see page 15)—one that rivals the blue whale, thought to be the largest living thing on Earth, even beyond the dinosaur. New analysis even suggests that the Michigan fungus may actually be almost twice as old and twice as large as originally thought!

The honey mushroom, once at home in its rotting-tree environment, is responsible for the condition known as foxfire, first recorded by Aristotle in 382 BCE, as it eerily glows in the dark (see page 33 for more), lighting the night for forest creatures and other inhabitants. While mysterious, the glow is actually produced from a chemical reaction between a molecule called luciferin and oxygen.

Certain orchid seedlings that begin their life underground are nourished by honey mushrooms' mycelial root systems until they emerge above ground and can photosynthesize their own foods to grow and bloom into the glorious forest dwellers they are.

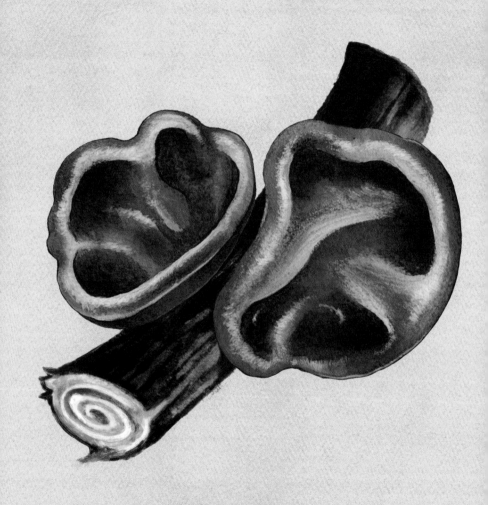

Auricularia auricula, Auricularia auricula-judae

Wood Ear

EDIBILITY ⁘ Edible, mainly for texture, with no real discernible flavor.

MANIFESTING INFLUENCE ⁘ Accountability, grounding, listening and communication.

OTHER COMMON NAMES ⁘ Cloud ear, jelly ear, Judas's ear.

L**ISTEN UP!** Common in many parts of Europe, especially Britain and Ireland, as well as North America, Asia, and Australia, the wood ear is widely used in culinary applications for its jelly-like texture, especially in Asian cuisines. It bears an uncanny resemblance to a wrinkly human ear. The wood ear is found growing on trees, most typically the elder tree, which you may remember as the tree from which Judas Iscariot hanged himself in shame following his betrayal of Christ. The elder has ever since borne these ear-shaped growths—some say as a curse—and the mushrooms, according to folklore, are evidence of Judas's returning spirit and a reminder of his betrayal and death.

A folk medicine staple, this mushroom has been used to treat simple things like earaches and sore throats to more complex conditions like jaundice, tumor growth, and cholesterol. The Chinese often include wood ear in dishes for its believed ability to improve breathing, circulation, and overall well-being. In recent medicine, studies are promising in showing wood ear's ability to lower cholesterol and help treat cancer and diabetes, among other conditions. All things worth listening to.

Cantharellus cibarius

Chanterelle

EDIBILITY ✥ Edible, and very tasty; typically ranked in the top five of edible mushrooms for its fruity—almost of apricot—slightly peppery flavor and distinctive sweetest-smelling-flower aroma. Beware of poisonous false species.

MANIFESTING INFLUENCE ✥ Abundance, good health, happiness, self-esteem, Sun magic, wealth.

OTHER COMMON NAMES ✥ Girolle, golden chanterelle.

TRUMPETING SUMMER, this stunner appears like wildflowers all over the world (except Antarctica and Greenland) and competition for her affection is fierce, as the chanterelle only grows in the wild. Oak and conifer forests are a favored haunt, where chanterelles establish their symbiotic relationships with the trees that allow them to populate the forest floor in clusters with abandon. A relative of the black trumpet mushroom, it's said you can identify the golden chanterelle from its delightful sweet fruity scent alone (but, of course, you wouldn't do that before eating any, just to be safe!). The chanterelle has a wavy funnel shape and its golden hue is like a ray of sunshine—together vaguely reminiscent of a zucchini blossom. There are actually more than ninety species in this family of mushrooms, and records reflect that the chanterelle was enjoyed and eaten as far back as the sixteenth century; but it was especially favored by the nobility, giving it an air of exclusivity and making it a symbol of wealth.

No matter where you live, locals proclaim that their chanterelles are tastiest. And not only is eating chanterelles good for your taste buds, it can also be good for your health. It is known that the chanterelle has antibacterial, antioxidant, and antiviral properties and is loaded with eight of the nine essential amino acids the body needs to thrive.

Clathrus archeri

Devil's Fingers

EDIBILITY ⁘ Young egg stage only, if you dare.

MANIFESTING INFLUENCE ⁘ Courage, expanding your reach, getting noticed, grabbing what you want.

OTHER COMMON NAMES ⁘ Octopus stinkhorn, squidward mushroom, starfish fungus.

A CHANCE ENCOUNTER with this slime-bearing, malodorous, creepy creature could certainly make you believe in the Devil. Burning-red, gnarly, slime-covered fingers, rising, reaching out among the leaf litter beckoning you near—threatening to pull you under with it! But wait, that dreaded evil, rotting flesh "stink" should warn you away.

The Devil's free-moving fingers (four to eight in all) unfurl, hatching from a leathery egg, from summer to fall like other stinkhorns (pages 151 and 153), into a starfish-like shape, making itself available for those spore-spreading flies to reach its slimy digits and thus continue to seed the next creepy generation of this terrifying stinkhorn. And despite the bright color and fantastic shape, it is the horrific smell that attracts the flies—they smell dinner, whereas we smell something highly unappetizing.

Indigenous to New Zealand and Australia, this distinctly spooky specimen haunts North America, Europe, Britain, and Asia as well, thought to have been introduced to Europe in contaminated wool sent from Australia as part of World War I supplies. Though the devil's fingers are said to do good work in terms of breaking down organic matter to replenish the soil, they are definitely the stuff of horror-filled nightmares. Beware, lest your paths cross darkly in the night.

Clavaria zollingeri

Violet Coral

EDIBILITY ⋅⁘⋅ Edible, in small quantities, tasting of radish
or cucumber, but with a laxative effect.

MANIFESTING INFLUENCE ⋅⁘⋅ Cosmic energy, intuition,
self-confidence, wisdom.

OTHER COMMON NAMES ⋅⁘⋅ Magenta coral.

THIS STUNNING, deeply violet-hued mushroom transports you to an undersea world on dry land. Looking entirely like sea coral, this fairy club fungus can almost always be found lying on moss under hardwood trees or in unimproved grassy areas. It grows as a single specimen, though sometimes in small groups, in summer through fall, most commonly in eastern North America, but it has been found in other places in the world, such as Scotland and Wales, Australia and New Zealand, and South America and Asia. Widespread sightings are rare, and its appearance is fleeting, lasting only from a few days to a week. The undulating branches aren't just for swaying in the breeze; they elevate the spores, increasing the chances they'll be spread over a wider area in which to reproduce.

Although rated as edible, its culinary value is negligible, so any specimens found should be enjoyed for their visual beauty and left, respectfully, to grow happily in their found location and continue their job in Nature's nutrient cycle. Pause for a moment to absorb the purple-hued energies and feel a lift in your mood, and know that a sighting such as this puts you in rarified company, indeed, so be grateful for the lucky experience.

Coprinellus disseminatus

Fairy Inkcap

EDIBILITY ⁘ Thought to be edible, but not confirmed, and usually discounted as to its culinary value.

MANIFESTING INFLUENCE ⁘ Friendship, happiness, healing, individuality, intuition, security.

OTHER COMMON NAMES ⁘ Fairies bonnets, trooping crumble cap, trooping inkcap.

E ASILY RECOGNIZED and found the world over, the diminutive, delightful fairy inkcap is straight out of a fairy tale, where it would be at home among the trooping fairies, for it's usually found in surprisingly large groups, populating remnants of rotting tree stumps and roots. The fairy inkcap's ability to derive nutrients from decaying matter, which it also helps recycle, speaks to its energies of lessons learned and used for growth, and the ability to let go of what no longer serves.

What the fairy inkcap lacks in stature it makes up for in sheer numbers, sprouting from early spring to winter and forming gregarious crowds of small white specimens. As the fairy inkcap ages (within just a few days), its white cap begins to turn gray and blacken at the edges, but it does not dissolve into total black inkiness as others in this family do. Rarely found alone, a sighting can foretell of new friendships.

Their small (½ inch, or 1 centimeter) bell-shaped caps with delicate, deeply pleated gills—perfect for adorning any fairy's head—are held aloft on slender stems. They are very fragile, disintegrating on touch, and best handled only by fairies. If you close your eyes and listen carefully, you may hear the choir of fairy bells ringing its greeting in the morning.

Coprinus comatus

Shaggy Inkcap

EDIBILITY ❖ When young only and within an hour or two of gathering or it may self-destruct before your eyes! And never with alcohol.

MANIFESTING INFLUENCE ❖ Banishing, leadership, protection, selflessness, truth.

OTHER COMMON NAMES ❖ Inky cap, lawyer's wig, shaggy mane.

A BIT WICKED WITCH, a tad Hulk, and a modicum of *Mission: Impossible*, this conspicuous fungus looks more like a drum major's hat than a mushroom. Its tall size (4 to 8 inches, or 10 to 20 centimeters) makes it easily spotted among meadows, woods, and roadsides throughout mainland Europe and parts of North America. In fact, it's fairly indiscriminate about where it grows—even, literally, breaking through asphalt and concrete when needed to continue its march.

The initial white egg form of this fungus morphs into a long bell shape, covered in brown-tipped, shaggy, wooly "hairs" or "scales." As it matures, getting hairier and shaggier in the process, the bell shape shortens to a bell cap set upon the stem. The gills, white initially, turn pink, then eventually blacken and liquefy from the edges into a black, inky, mess, dripping slime—and spores—until the mushroom almost seems to melt, leaving behind the stem alone and the question as to whether or not it was ever really there! Rather than melt, though, the mushroom is actually digesting itself in order to release its spores in a process called deliquescence.

In fact, the liquid was used, back in the seventeenth and eighteenth centuries, as an ink substitute. It was even proposed that the ink, full of fungal spores, be used for important documents—lack of any spores would clearly reveal a forgery!

If you're so inclined, use shaggy inkcap's ability to melt into nothing as a visualization exercise to melt away any troubles keeping you up at night, or harness the ink and use it to write your intentions in your journal.

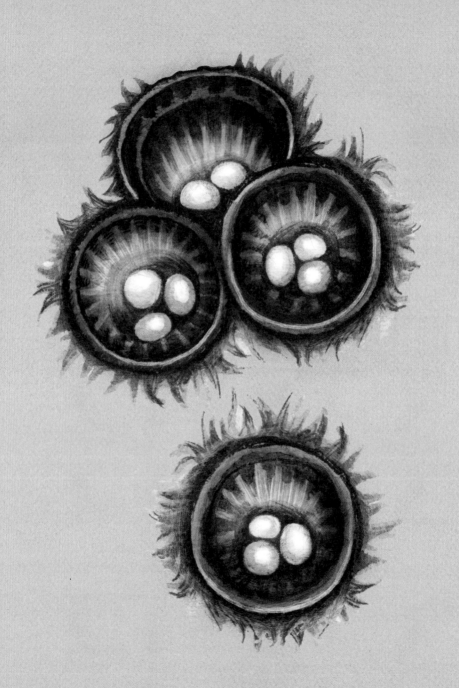

Cyathus striatus

Bird's Nest Fungus

EDIBILITY ⁘ Inedible.

MANIFESTING INFLUENCE ⁘ Adaptation, creativity, fertility, intuition, mindful existence, protection.

OTHER COMMON NAMES ⁘ Elfin cups, fairy goblets, fluted bird's nest, pixie's purses, splash cups.

Found all over the world, this tiny charmer is actually quite complex. This delicate mushroom, which is shaped like a trumpet, looks exactly like a tiny bird's nest cradling its precious eggs. The "eggs" are actually spore sacs, or periodoles, containing millions of spores, and a single nest can hold up to twenty of these. The spores are dispersed by raindrops, which splash them out of and away from—up to 6 feet (1.8 meters)—the "nest." Interestingly, in the eighteenth century, before our knowledge of mushrooms grew, the spore sacs were misidentified as seeds (and at one time were thought to sprout into birds when nourished by the Sun!). The spores are equipped with a sort of bungee cord (the funiculus), which helps them find and attach to a new food source once out of the nest (just like a momma bird!).

The shaggy mushroom cup, or nest, even has a lid to protect the spores until they are ripe and ready to leave. Colors can range from bright orange to dull brown. They're most commonly spotted in fall in large clusters on dead and decaying wood and wood mulch but can be found year-round in more temperate areas. Though widespread, their small size and camouflaging colors can make sightings difficult. If you spot one, make a wish, as fairies are nearby.

Current research indicates this small mushroom could have a mighty impact on inhibiting pancreatic cancer growth.

King Alfred's Cakes

EDIBILITY ⁘ Inedible.

MANIFESTING INFLUENCE ⁘ Destruction and renewal, protection.

OTHER COMMON NAMES ⁘ Carbon ball, coal fungus, cramp balls.

LOOKING RATHER like small lumps of coal and found growing on decaying wood (typically ash) over a period of many years, this interesting mushroom gets its name from a tale about the ninth-century Anglo-Saxon King Alfred. Searching to escape capture by the Vikings, the king was given refuge by a simple peasant woman, who (not knowing he was king) tasked Alfred with keeping an eye on the cakes baking in the hearth. The results were less than edible (he was probably preoccupied with being captured by the fearsome enemy) and it is said, in his embarrassment, he scattered the burnt cakes in the forest to dispense with the evidence.

Also called a "fire lighter," the young pinkish-brown mushrooms develop their black shiny patina, revealing striking silver rings inside when cut open, each representing a season of reproduction as they age. Mature mushrooms can serve as a fire starter and they smolder, burning slowly, like the coal they resemble. Evidence of their use for such purposes dates back to a seven-thousand-year-old Spanish settlement, leading to speculation that this fact could have even been known as far back as during the Stone Age, when our ancestors may even have used the mushroom to transport fires, and means of making fire, from one location to another. You'll find these mushrooms commonly in Britain and Ireland, as well as Australia, Europe, and North America.

Their unusual common name of "cramp balls" originates with the belief that carrying these mushrooms around under your arms, or placing them between the sheets if bedridden, would relieve one of cramps. How they caused relief is still somewhat of a mystery!

Entoloma hochstetteri

Werewere-Kōkăko

EDIBILITY ❖ Unknown, but likely poisonous.

MANIFESTING INFLUENCE ❖ Patience, sincerity, speaking your truth, standing out in a crowd.

OTHER COMMON NAMES ❖ Blue pinkgill, sky-blue mushroom.

THIS BEAUTY, native to New Zealand—so iconic it graces their $50 note and thus the only mushroom to be featured on any currency worldwide—carries the Māori name *werewere-kōkako* because its glorious indigo-blue color reminds you of the striking blue wattle of the endangered kōkako bird. Māori lore tells us that the mushroom came first, though, noting the bird acquired its lovely markings by rubbing its cheek up against one of the mushrooms. Nature doesn't give us many true-blue items, especially plants, so this lovely stands out among the other inhabitants of the forest floor between January and July. The entire mushroom is blue: cap, stem, and gills, but the spores give it a reddish-pink tinge underneath.

In its search for natural food dyes to supplant synthetic ones consumers dislike, the multi billion-dollar global food industry, using research from the University of Auckland on microbe-derived pigments, including from *Entoloma hochstetteri*, may be on to something. And, uncovering the secrets of the mushroom's blue hue could solve the problem of the missing blue Froot Loops in some countries, where they're banned from the box because their dyes may be potentially harmful.

Because of its relative rarity, not much is known scientifically about *Entoloma hochstetteri*. The biologic purpose for its blue hue isn't precisely known, either: It could attract potential pollinators to spread its spores or warn away those creatures who may do it harm. Energetically, it sings of the freedom to be you, uniquely you, and unafraid to stand out in a crowd.

Geastrum spp.

Earthstar

EDIBILITY ⁘ Inedible.

MANIFESTING INFLUENCE ⁘ Adaptation, astral travel, fertility.

OTHER COMMON NAMES ⁘ Collared earthstar, true earthstar.

T HERE ARE MORE than sixty species of this uniquely shaped mushroom found in wooded areas the world over, fruiting in fall, sometimes through winter. All feature a puffball-like spore sac that almost resembles an acorn held aloft like a treasure by the surrounding "petals," or rays, of the mushroom that have peeled away from the sac, so the spores can catch the breeze—or a raindrop—in order to release. The petals form a star shape, which gives this easily recognizable mushroom its common name. Earthstars release their spores in a similar way to puffballs (page 135), hopefully landing in fertile conditions to produce more constellations of little earthstars. Their slightly alien appearance may have inspired a seventeenth-century botanical illustration, humorously titled *Fungus anthropomorphos*, depicting the center sac as a ring of humans (ring around the earthstar, anyone?), and, sometime in the 1860s, a forward-thinking English mushroom scholar is said to have proclaimed that these heavenly specimens, on occasion, seek to leave their Earthly realm (prompted by a recently discovered earthstar on the tallest of spires adorning London's St. Paul's Cathedral!).

There is another earthstar of the *Astraeus* family, *Astraeus hygrometricus*, also called the barometer earthstar or false earthstar, that displays an uncommon ability to predict the weather. These little treasures open and close in relation to moisture: lots of moisture—open; not so much—close.

Though probably not found far from Earth, earthstars can sometimes be found populating a fairy ring. If you stumble upon one, thank your lucky stars and make a wish upon one.

Gliophorus psittacinus

Parrot Waxcap

EDIBILITY ⁘ Debated, but the mushrooms are small and slimy, with little taste or aroma, so not the most appetizing choice, and their increasing rarity speaks to respectfully leaving them where found, thriving in their natural habitat.

MANIFESTING INFLUENCE ⁘ Beauty, good luck, self-reliance, success.

OTHER COMMON NAMES ⁘ Parrot mushroom, parrot toadstool.

THIS SMALL, beautiful umbrella-shaped mushroom glistens like glass while putting on a colorful display. The hues are quite distinctive in the mushroom's early stages: the emerald to dark to olive green cap, with shades of yellow, orange, or purple, atop a yellow stem, mimicking the parrot's magnificent plumage for which it's named. Still lovely as it ages, the parrot waxcap changes from shades of pink to yellow to orange, like tropical feathers and foliage, and finally fades into a nondescript unnoticed mushroom in the woods. (Ah, the march of time!) And true to its name, this mushroom has a waxy texture owing to the sticky, gluey, slimy substance that coats the cap, gills, and stem.

Though rather reclusive, the parrot waxcap can be found commonly in the United Kingdom, across Europe though becoming rarer, and in the United States, typically through fall into winter. It favors cooler climates and a variety of habitats—from grasslands to forests to mossy groves and roadsides—though it prefers soils that have not been altered with fertilizers or pesticides and does not like to be disturbed once established.

Grifola frondosa

Maitake

EDIBILITY ⁘ A choice edible, highly valued for its delicious flavor, earthy aroma, and meaty texture; maitake brings an umami flavor, or fifth taste, to foods.

MANIFESTING INFLUENCE ⁘ Adaptation, good luck, health, joy, power.

OTHER COMMON NAMES ⁘ Dancing mushroom, hen-of-the-woods, king of mushrooms, sheep's head, the unmarried woman.

NATIVE TO CHINA, Eastern North America, and parts of Japan, this smoky brown mushroom grows in large clumps, or rosettes, near the base of oak trees, where it feeds on the tree's dead roots. Called the "dancing mushroom" by the Japanese, this name is derived from a folk story found in the eleventh-century Japanese folktale collection called *Konjaku monogatari* (*Tales of Long Ago*) that tells the story of a group of woodcutters lost in the Kitayama Mountains searching for their way home, who encounter a group of lost nuns gleefully dancing and singing (likely demons, they think!), also searching for their way home. When they meet, warily, the nuns explain their search for flowers to honor Buddha caused them to become lost—and hungry—but they found mushrooms, which they ate, and enjoyed, but which caused them to dance uncontrollably. The woodcutters, being hungry, too, ask for a bite, and they, too, dance with glee. From then on the mushroom was known as "maitake," or dancing mushroom.

Others say the name derives from the mushroom hunter's leap for good luck that erupts on discovery of this (previously) rare mushroom. And, quite appropriately, maitake's wavy undulating feathery form actually mimics a skirt atwirl in dance and could be said to be dancing itself.

Maitake's size can be massive, sometimes weighing up to 50 pounds (22.5 kilograms), and its locations in the wild, where the mushrooms are known to reappear annually in fall, are often closely guarded family secrets.

Hericium erinaceus

Lion's Mane

EDIBILITY ⁙ Edible, with a taste, it's said, that's similar to crab.

MANIFESTING INFLUENCE ⁙ Clarity of thought, concentration, courage and vigor, Moon magic, remembrance, spiritual wisdom.

OTHER COMMON NAMES ⁙ Bearded tooth, icicle mushroom, monkey's head, old man's beard, pom pom, tree hedgehog fungus, yamabushitake mushroom.

B**ARELY EVEN** recognizable as a mushroom, this formidable tooth fungus gets its name from the long, white, shaggy, hairlike structures on its body that call to mind the magnificent male lion's mane. Though fierce in appearance, their texture is described as bendable, like rubber. The mushroom itself looks a bit like cauliflower when cut into cross sections, with its mainly white to cream color speaking of clairvoyance and truth.

Lion's mane is found in North America, Asia, and Europe, from late summer into fall, typically growing on hardwoods in old, established forests, especially oak and beech. This mushroom typically grows higher up on the tree than other mushrooms, which makes this rare beauty even harder to spot.

Its medicinal properties have been known and used as a tonic in traditional Chinese medicine for centuries, especially to prevent digestive issues, and Chinese folklore said nerves of steel were granted to any who ate this feral fungus. Lion's mane was revered by Buddhist monks for its ability to instill quiet powers of concentration. Some current research has shown that lion's mane can actually stimulate nerves to regrow, suggesting it may be beneficial to treating Alzheimer's disease and other neurological health conditions, in addition to the antibacterial and anti-inflammatory properties it exhibits. The next time you're in the forest, listen for its roar!

Hydnellum peckii

Devil's Tooth

EDIBILITY ❖ Not poisonous but not really edible, either, due to its unpleasant taste.

MANIFESTING INFLUENCE ❖ Cooperation, irresistible charm, look beneath the surface for the true meaning, portends drama, success.

OTHER COMMON NAMES ❖ Bleeding tooth fungus, red-juice tooth, strawberries and cream fungus.

VARIOUSLY DESCRIBED as straight out of a horror movie or resembling a Danish pastry, this striking—whether beautiful or frighteningly gruesome is in the eye of the beholder—mushroom can be elusive, hiding among the leaves, mosses, and needles shed by the forest as it sleeps and wakes. But when found young, its lovely white-to-pinkish-hued cap often boasts patches of oozing deep-red liquid, a sort of sap, that can resemble strawberry jam—or blood. This strong red hue is a color that manifests as passion, love, courage, and power.

The liquid exudes from the mushroom in very damp, wet conditions, almost like it can't absorb any more from its surroundings. Its cap, too, is covered in fine hairlike structures, giving it a velvety touch, if you dare! It is typically found in woodlands in Scotland, Europe, and North America in late summer and fall, where it grows in symbiotic relation to the surrounding plants, typically conifers.

The underside of the mushroom's cap features spiny toothlike extensions—hence the name—rather than gills or pores, which is where the spores develop.

The mushroom is valued for its use in making natural dyes. It is also thought to have anticoagulant properties, which keep your blood flowing, as well as being antibacterial. Devil's tooth also contains the chemical thelephoric acid, which may someday help take a bite out of Alzheimer's disease.

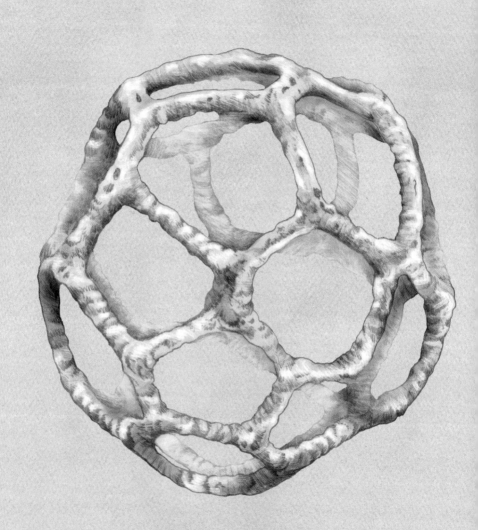

Ileodictyon cibarium

Basket Fungus

EDIBILITY ❖ At the immature egg stage only, but not recommended or known for certain. (Do you want to be the first to confirm this?!)

MANIFESTING INFLUENCE ❖ Establishing boundaries, freedom, self-knowledge, truth, transparency.

OTHER COMMON NAMES ❖ Common basket stinkhorn, stink cage, white basket fungus, wrinkled cage.

Found primarily in New Zealand and Australia, this uniquely shaped, white, cage-like mushroom is rather alien-looking and a bit too geometrically symmetrical to be real. It's fun to look at but don't get too close: it's also rather foul-smelling and covered in a greenish-brown slime. The Māori people in what is now known as New Zealand had thirty-five different names for this mushroom, including many reflecting its sudden and mysterious appearance, such as "star poo" and "ghost dung," as well as "house of the Devil," and "lightning droppings," which references Whaitiri, the goddess of thunder, because of the mushroom's tendency to sprout unexplainably following thunderstorms.

The mushroom fruits year-round on decaying and dead organic matter in garden mulch, along the roadside, in cultivated areas, and in woods and forests. It begins looking like a puffball (page 135), but as it grows, it bursts into the enchanting open-weave soccer-ball shape ranging in size from 2 to 10 inches (5 to 25 centimeters) across. When mature, it breaks away from its base and tumbles off in the wind, scattering its spores along the way.

There are other similar mushrooms in other parts of the world, such as the *Clathrus ruber*, or red cage fungus, which vary in color but share the lattice-like structure, stinkhorn origins and characteristics, and fascinatingly marvelous representation of Nature's wonder.

Amethyst Deceiver

EDIBILITY ✣ Caps are technically edible if positively identified (stems are fibrous) but the taste is nothing special; their small size means you need a lot to make a meal; they can cause gastric upset; they will absorb arsenic from soil, if present.

MANIFESTING INFLUENCE ✣ Adaptation to change, beauty, intuition, patience, protection, self-assurance.

OTHER COMMON NAMES ✣ Red cabbage fungus.

S TRAIGHT OUT of a fairy tale, this diminutive beauty is a bit of a trickster personality: a stunning violet color when wet, the amethyst deceiver turns a rather pale gray–buff color, almost white, when dry, making identification tricky—and even more so considering the undulating changes in appearance as the mushroom ages—thus the "deceiver" moniker. It was described first by English botanist William Hudson in 1778.

The amethyst deceiver is at home among northern woodlands in Asia, Europe, and North America. Growing from late summer to early winter, it remains almost unnoticed among the leaf litter—but look closely near beech or oak trees and you may find this lovely waiting to be discovered. The charming silky cap, which is concave when young, with its thick purple gills would make delightful fairy haberdashery, or a good place to hide from the rain. And like the fairies it delights, it can be found as a solitary specimen or in small troops in clusters. Despite the delightful violet color, this mushroom's spores are white.

Spying this purple people pleaser is a glimpse of Nature's magic. Its energies can help ease times of change and open our minds to new experiences. Like the amethyst stone whose name it bears, this mushroom is a true jewel of the forest.

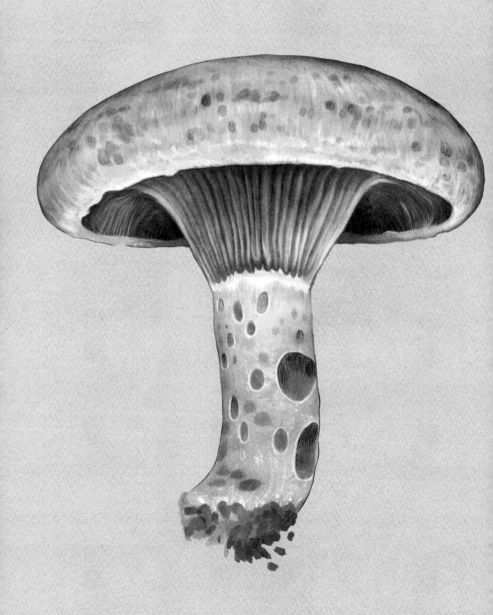

Lactarius indigo

Indigo Milk Cap

EDIBILITY ✣ Edible.

MANIFESTING INFLUENCE ✣ Clear communication, patience, tranquility.

OTHER COMMON NAMES ✣ Blue milk mushroom, indigo mushroom.

T HIS MUSHROOM is an attention-getter for all the right reasons. Another stunning blue beauty (see werewere-kōkako on page 113) that reminds us of the magnificence of Nature, the indigo milk cap, a member of the genus *Lactarius*, shares this group's common characteristic of the ability to ooze "milk" (latex) once bruised or broken, sometimes called lactating. But the indigo milk cap's milk is special and definitely not something to cry over: It's blue, turning dark green when exposed to the air. It's also not as abundant as some others in this group.

More alien landscape than forest woodscape, you'll frequently find this medium-size mushroom specimen growing in oak and pine forests across China, North America (especially in Mexico), and South America, from about midsummer to early fall, forming symbiotic relationships with the trees in a beneficial exchange of nutrients. And though rare, you don't have to wait 'til the next Blue Moon to go in search of its inspiration.

The indigo milk cap's cap is initially dome-shaped, flattening and spreading up to 6 inches (15 centimeters) wide as it matures.

There aren't many naturally blue foods, but this edible one is said to be delicious (though that perception may be influenced by its glorious color: We eat first with our eyes!)—and the bluer the mushroom, the fresher it is.

Let the soothing indigo hue of this mushroom awaken your inner intuition and transport you to a place of peace and tranquility.

Laetiporus sulphureus

Chicken-of-the-Woods

EDIBILITY ⁂ Although edible when cooked, some people experience allergic reactions to eating it. Be wary, and never eat any mushroom unless you are beyond certain of what you have.

MANIFESTING INFLUENCE ⁂ Ambition, change, good luck, happiness.

OTHER COMMON NAMES ⁂ Chicken fungus, chicken mushroom, crab-of-the-woods, yellow sulfur shelf.

WHAT A SIGHT in the woods this mushroom must have been to French botanist Jean Baptiste François (Pierre) Bulliard, who first described this beauty in 1798. To many, this fan-shaped edible mushroom (of which there are numerous species), when eaten young, actually tastes like and resembles the texture of chicken—hence the common name. (Not to be confused with hen-of-the-woods, or the maitake, on page 119.) It's usually found in late summer to early fall growing horizontally in a manner called shelving or bracketing, in clusters on dead or mature wood, mostly oak, around the globe. These mushrooms can grow quite large—up to 20 inches (50 centimeters) across. The largest known specimen, found in the United Kingdom, tipped the scales at 100 pounds (45 kilograms). They are a striking orange-coral color with a suede-like feel and call to mind flower petals in shape. Their lovely color, which fades as the mushroom ages, can also be used as a natural dye, and speaks of manifesting energies of ambition, warmth, good health, and joy.

Chicken-of-the-woods has a long history in European folk medicine traditions, being used to treat a variety of infections. Romanian folklore holds that eating chicken-of-the-woods in spring brings good luck.

Although a delicacy in some parts of the world, it is an unwanted resident in others due to its tendency to cause wood rot.

Lentinula edodes

Shiitake

EDIBILITY ✣ Highly prized for its distinct smoky, earthy, umami flavor and firm, meaty texture, making it an excellent stand-in for meat.

MANIFESTING INFLUENCE ✣ Grounding, health, longevity, romance, vitality.

OTHER COMMON NAMES ✣ Forest mushroom, king of mushrooms, oak mushroom, perfumed mushroom.

MUSHROOM CULTIVATION likely started in China and Japan more than one thousand years ago where observers noted the native shiitake mushroom growing in the wild, from spring to early fall, on decaying shii trees (a type of oak from which the mushroom gets its name) and discovered that when they placed more logs among the mushroom-growing logs, shiitakes sprouted there, too. The first written record of shiitake cultivation appears in the Song dynasty (960–1129 CE) and is credited to Wu San Kwung, creator of the process, who is honored by a temple devoted to him in every mushroom-growing village in China. Today, shiitakes are the second most cultivated mushroom in the world and a multibillion-dollar industry per the USDA.

This tan to dark-brown mushroom with a wide cap is the predominant mushroom used in Japanese and Chinese cooking. Additionally, in Japanese culture, shiitake was believed to be a potent aphrodisiac. So revered was it, that it is frequently depicted being held by deities in ancient tapestries, artwork, and manuscripts.

Its history in Asian folk medicine is long and its healing powers wide-ranging. Even today, in many parts of Asia, shiitake is regarded as a medicinal food and eaten regularly as part of a daily diet. Modern science may have found evidence that shiitakes are effective at fighting certain cancers and lowering serum cholesterol as well, spurring further study. Shiitakes may even be a source of biofuel.

Lycoperdon perlatum (common puffball),
Calvatia, Calvatia gigantea

Puffball

EDIBILITY ⁘ Young mushrooms are edible, though
only after conclusive identification.

MANIFESTING INFLUENCE ⁘ Bringing out the hidden truth, intuition,
peace, protection from evil, seeing what's in plain sight.

OTHER COMMON NAMES ⁘ Common puffball, Devil's snuffbox,
giant puffball, Puck's stool, wolf fart.

T HE PUFFBALL gets its name rather mundanely, but it is a sight to
see: when the fruiting body (the ball) bursts, it expels visible clouds
of spores forcefully into the air through an opening that has developed
at the top of the ball—like magical mushroom fairy dust. It's interesting
to note, too, that the puffball, in England, was also known as pixie puff.
Another fantastical common name, wolf fart, is a literal translation of the
Latin *Lycoperdon*: *Lyco*, from the Greek, means "wolf"; *perdon* means "to
break wind." Sometimes the obvious name is the best!

True puffballs do not have a stalk, or stem; other puffball types do.
They range in size from a golf ball to a soccer ball, with some big enough
to sit on, like the giant puffball, *Calvatia gigantea*. Common in the United
Kingdom from July to November, this white globe of firm flesh can grow
to 3 feet (1 meter) across and weigh up to 25 pounds (11 kilograms). Huge
fairy rings made up of fifty or more giant puffballs have been found in
various locations. The white flesh of a young puffball is edible, but not
to be gathered in the wild without knowing what you have, as it can be
confused with similar-looking, but poisonous, mushrooms.

The ball turns into a huge spore sac as it matures. One estimate of the
number of spores contained within a 15-inch (38 centimeters) puffball is

seven trillion! And as mushroom luck would have it, this beauty grows in forests, grassy areas like lawns, golf courses, and pastures, and even by roadsides, where the spores land when they are released from the ball. Just the slightest touch of a raindrop or the whisper of a breeze is enough to set the process in motion.

Many Indigenous Peoples of North America believed that puffballs, burned as incense, defended against ghosts and other spirits, or could warn them away when the puffballs were dried, filled with small stones, tied to the end of sticks, and rattled. They believed puffballs could also serve as talismans and good luck charms, wearing them dried on necklaces for such purpose. The Blackfoot called them fallen stars, thought them a source of supernatural occurrences, and dried and burned them as tinder for life-giving fire. The Cherokee used the spores to cure burns and sores. In rural America, burning the common puffball was a way to sedate bees so honey could be safely retrieved from their hives. This practice led to research about the possible sedative effects this mushroom could offer.

Their white color and circular shape speak of peace and unending potential.

Marasmius oreades

Fairy Ring Mushroom

EDIBILITY ⊹ Yes, but never assume any mushroom, growing in a fairy ring or not, is edible without an expert's identification.

MANIFESTING INFLUENCE ⊹ Adaptation, connections, merriment, second chances.

OTHER COMMON NAMES ⊹ Common toadstool, fairy ring champignon, pixie stool, Scotch bonnet.

O F THE VAST number of classified mushroom species, it is believed that hundreds are capable of producing the delightful fairy ring, but the most well known is the *Marasmius oreades*—or the aptly named fairy ring mushroom or fairy ring champignon—native to North America and Europe. They grow in grassy areas, such as lawns, parks, golf courses, and meadows, and as we know from exploring fairy rings in more detail (see page 31), their complex mycelium grows in an outward circular pattern as it searches for food, causing the distinctive dark-green ring of grass enclosing an area that looks fairy-trampled, brown, and less than healthy, where the mushrooms' "roots" and the roots of the grass compete for water and nutrients. This last fact, unfortunately, is what makes this particular mushroom a bane to manicured lawns everywhere: It is the only fairy ring mushroom to create such destruction. Their rings can live for hundreds of years, expanding in area each year, depending on growing conditions.

Each summer, these small, creamy-colored, broadly round-capped mushrooms sporting pleated gills sprout from the healthy, growing mycelium living underneath the green grass. When the mushrooms sprout, the fae folk come out to frolic!

Despite the numerous origin theories of the mysterious fairy ring—which, in addition to fairy feet, witches, and dragons, have been credited to aliens, snail slime, the propensity of moles to burrow in circles and their resulting dung residue, cattle dung, rutting deer, and goat dung—in 1792, English physician and amateur botanist William Withering broke the magic spell when he correctly identified the fairy ring mushroom as its rightful source.

The real magic of these mushrooms may not lie within the fairy ring, though, but rather in their unusual ability to resurrect themselves. These mushrooms will shrivel and "die" in the heat of the Sun, then exhibit the unusual ability of "coming back to life" when doused with water, as by a passing rain shower—even being able to produce new spores on revival, over multiple "lives." They contain a sugar called trehalose, which seems to act as a protectant to the mushroom's cells on dehydration, then dissolves in the rainwater to feed the cells and nourish them back to life, stimulating them to divide and grow.

The mushroom, *Marasmius oreades*, is edible and prized for its slightly sweet taste, likely from the sugar. Traditional Chinese medicine recognizes its ability to ease joint pain and inflammation. But remember, never eat any mushrooms unless you know EXACTLY what you've got, as some fairy ring mushrooms look similar but are irreversibly poisonous.

Morchella spp.

Morel

EDIBILITY ⁘ Edible, when cooked; highly prized for its meaty texture and complex, earthy, nutty flavor. Some people are allergic. Beware the false morel, for it is poisonous.

MANIFESTING INFLUENCE ⁘ Destruction, letting go so new growth may emerge, teamwork.

OTHER COMMON NAMES ⁘ Dryland fish, hickory chickens, merkels (miracles), molly moochers.

A LONG WITH the Sabbat of Ostara, which marks the spring equinox, another of the most-anticipated first indications that spring has sprung is the reemergence of the morels from the sleepy forest floor. Not "technically" a mushroom—it has neither gills nor pores—though it is a fungus, the morel is related to the truffle (page 175). The morel also grows in the moist soils of the forests, exhibiting particularly finicky preferences for just the right growing conditions. A favorite of Louis XIII, he was known to happily string them for drying in his bedroom, for he so loved their woodsy scent, and was said to be engaged in such activity at the time of his death. Morels can often be found beneath specific types of trees, where they act as decayers. In symbiosis with the apple tree, the morel speaks of love; with ash, of love, prosperity, health, intuition; with elm, the favorite tree of elves, also of love, communicating with other realms, grounding, and compassion; with oak, of protection, home, and fame. Its colors of yellow and black lend the magical energies of confidence, joy, success, healing, protection, and security.

Though elusive, the morel is sought after in a rather cult-like way, spawning expeditions, festivals, championships, pre- and post-exploration rituals, and more. It is the most recognizable, and most delectable, of mushrooms, with the most common ones being black and yellow, with their suggestive shape, signature conical hollow cap that looks somewhat like a brain, attached at the base of the cap to a hollow stem. Generations of families carry on their tradition of hunting morel mushrooms with the best spots kept top secret and guarded fiercely (some even passed on in wills), though technological advancements now include apps where other successful hunters share the secrets to their bounty. (Another reminder here: always be sure you know what you have before eating any wild-gathered mushrooms.)

Despite the lack of sunshine in their growth habitat, and the inability to utilize sunshine for food production due to their lack of chlorophyll, morels are rich in vitamin D. Their rich meaty flavor and texture make a great low-cal alternative to meat and are a boon to those who choose not to eat meat for whatever reason. Morels emerge from the soil, seemingly full-grown, during spring months. Among the most expensive of mushrooms, their short growing season and unpredictable growth habits translate to hefty prices when purchased fresh—from $30 to $90 per pound (0.45 kilogram). They can also be purchased dried, and because it takes so many more when dried to equal a pound, have been known to sell for more than $250 per pound. Commercial ventures to grow morels have, so far, been largely unsuccessful.

In Eastern Europe, morels were, at one time, regarded as the work of the Devil. Today, Europeans' regard for the delicacy that is morels is high indeed, where it was routine at one time to set fire to wooded areas to encourage a lush growth of morels in spring—the ash seems to create the right soil conditions (alkaline) for the morels to thrive. In the Himalayas, it's believed morels spring forth when the Rain God is happiest, with a combination of rain, thunder, and lightning giving birth to a healthy crop. Perhaps an offering to the Rain God is in order.

MOREL MANIA

The delightfully delectable black morels, *Morchella angusticeps*, are the first to poke their heads from the thawing Earth, especially following a first rain, and when the nights are decidedly warmer (at least 50 degrees Fahrenheit, or 10 degrees Celsius), followed closely by the white variety, *Morchella esculenta*. The giant morels, *Morchella crassipes*, reaching 6 to 8 inches (15 to 20 centimeters) tall, are last.

When looking for morels, keep in mind that they like to establish symbiotic relationships with trees—especially those that are injured or dying—in their preferred habitat, mainly apple, ash, elm, oak, and tulip. Looking nearby these trees when out sleuthing is at least one way to increase your odds of finding these treasures. Another tip: Follow the dandelions. Once the dandelions have emerged, it's said the morels are not far behind.

The reward? Besides the tasty morel itself, once you discover a productive location, it's your secret to guard, as morels are known to return year after year for many years over, offering their tasty secrets to true believers. And, though disappointing, many a mushroom hunter does come home without the elusive treasure. However, the hunt is a supreme excuse for a meditative walk in the woods, as the Earth's returning to life, to boost your magical musings.

Omphalotus nidiformis

Ghost Fungus

EDIBILITY ⁜ Poisonous.

MANIFESTING INFLUENCE ⁜ Attraction, forgiveness, lighting the way, look beneath the surface, new ideas.

OTHER COMMON NAMES ⁜ Australian glow fungus.

A N ORDINARY beige mushroom by day, but one that glows spookily green at night, signals all may not be as it seems. This mysterious mushroom emits a bioluminescent, some say ghostly, glow. Native to Australia, these mushrooms can be found in fall after the rains, growing in forests, in clusters at the foot of trees, mainly in southern Australia and Tasmania. First Nations people in Australia associated them with evil spirits and the supernatural activity of their ancestors; in Micronesia, they were destroyed as bad omens and even used as body decoration to intimidate enemies. In the United States, California and Colorado miners feared them, as the glowing spots were thought to mark a fellow miner's death—perhaps even a sighting of his ghost! And everywhere, witches are drawn to them.

The real purpose of the mushroom's glow is not scientifically known. The common thought that the glow attracts insect pollinators was proven untrue in this case by a group of researchers at the University of Adelaide, but a more common theory is one worth considering: they safely light the way through the dark forest for any fairies, elves, or gnomes (or other nocturnal creatures) in transit. On a personal level, let the mushroom's glow remind you to let your light shine, for its unique energy may be just the beacon someone else needs to see.

If a search for these mesmerizing mushrooms is on your list, they're much more easily found during the day, then return at night when they reveal their magic.

Omphalotus olearius, O. illudens

Jack-o'-Lantern

EDIBILITY ⁘ Poisonous.

MANIFESTING INFLUENCE ⁘ Abundance, attraction, changing luck,
clear communication, courage, emotional healing, energy.

OTHER COMMON NAMES ⁘ False chanterelle.

JUST LIKE its Halloween namesake, this bright-orange jack-o'-lantern mushroom glows in the dark, exhibiting the eerie quality of bioluminescence (see page 33), lighting paths with a spooky greenish glow for all manner of haunted forest dweller, sometimes shining so brightly that you may spy a woodland elf reading a newspaper nearby. The fresher it is, the brighter it glows. The true reason for the glow is unknown, but scientists speculate it may attract insects to help spread its spores, creating more jack-o'-lantern pumpkin patches, or, in true jack-o'-lantern fashion, the glow may warn off predators and evil spirits.

Its appearance, from late summer to fall in Europe and North America, mysteriously coincides with Halloween and the increased nighttime sightings of fairies. By day, the large orange caps are regaled as among the most beautiful in the mushroom world—seemingly glowing in daylight as well.

They can sometimes be found in dazzling bouquets of hundreds of mushrooms feeding off dead trees and stumps when the growing conditions are just right. However, because of its resemblance to the edible chanterelle, mistakenly ingesting the jack-o'-lantern mushroom is one of the most common causes of mushroom poisoning—definitely more trick than treat. On the brighter side, though not edible, this mushroom is being studied for its cancer-fighting and cholesterol-lowering benefits and potential antibiotic properties, but nothing definitive has been proven.

Samhain is the perfect time to harvest this quite magical mushroom's energy to manifest intentions.

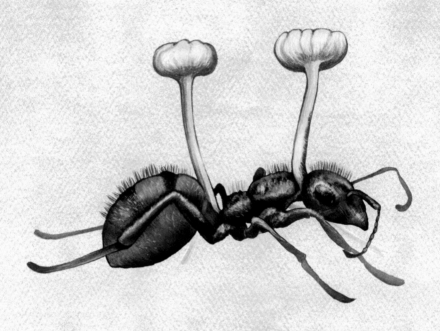

Ophiocordyceps unilateralis
Zombie Fungus

EDIBILITY ❖ Poisonous.

MANIFESTING INFLUENCE ❖ Adaptation, survival.

OTHER COMMON NAMES ❖ Zombie ant fungus.

IN THE SPIRIT of truth is stranger than fiction, and in this case science fiction, consider the zombie fungus, *Ophiocordyceps unilateralis*. Today, found mostly in tropical regions, this fungus quite literally takes control of an ant's body, eventually killing the ant by feeding on it.

The unsuspecting ant may just step on a fungal spore as it's out and about in the jungle. While the fungus is busy feeding on the ant's body and populating it with increasing numbers of fungal cells, the ant acts unaware, going about its daily ant business, to and from its home. Once the fungus has finished its feeding frenzy, it takes control of the ant's system (in this case, unzombie-like control of its muscles versus true zombie brain control), sending chemical signals to it that literally and specifically affect the ant's behavior: to leave the nest and climb a nearby plant—to a specific height—where the ant then locks its jaws on the plant and dies. But wait... the saga is not over: the fungus glues the ant's body to the leaf for stability, then produces a stalk that bursts forth from the ant's head, spewing reproductive spores all over the remaining ants' territory, initiating the dance all over again.

If that's not enough, hundreds of zombifying species of fungus are known, each with its own ant or insect species target, exhibiting tremendous evolutionary adaption through the millions of years they've existed. As yet, there is no known species of zombie fungus equipped to turn humans into zombies, which in today's lingo are aptly known as "the infected"!

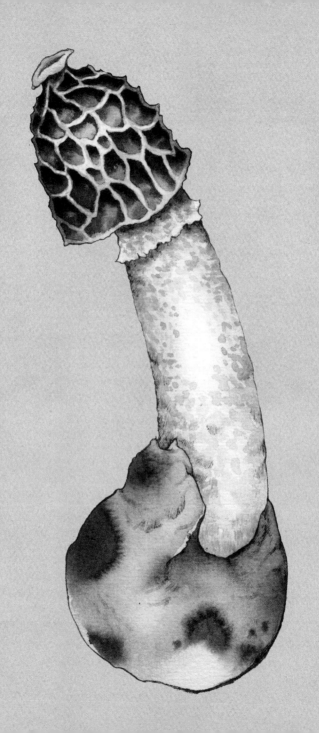

Phallus impudicus

Stinkhorn

EDIBILITY ⚜ Edible, only at the egg stage, but why would you?

MANIFESTING INFLUENCE ⚜ Assertiveness, attraction, compassion, growth, protection, vitality.

OTHER COMMON NAMES ⚜ Devil's egg, Devil's horn, Satan's member, witch's egg.

No TRYING to deny it, the stinkhorn, *Phallus impudicus*, is undeniably phallic in shape (to the amusement of many and the embarrassment of others!). Its inherently obscene nature was particularly offensive to the Victorians, who routinely took to warning young maidens from touching the offensive fungi.

The birth of this strange fungus, arising proudly, usually at night, witnessed only by the Moon, gave birth to some of its other common names, such as Devil's egg. Not shy by nature, this fantastical fungus grows fast enough to be observed—up to 4 inches (10 centimeters) per hour and growing up to 10 inches (25 centimeters) tall—and it's even said you can hear it growing, with sounds similar to the all-familiar "Snap! Crackle! Pop!" But that's only if you dare get close enough to listen. By morning, once fully (*ahem*) grown, it undergoes a series of chemical changes that produce a slimy olive-colored mass of spores on its cap that give it its namesake stink—of rotting flesh. You definitely don't want to get close enough for that and you'd likely have to fight off the flies, anyway.

The stinkhorn *Phallus impudicus* is not the singular example of obscenely shaped mushrooms, and stinkhorns also inhabit other shapes, such as starfish and squid. They all share, though, that odious odor that attracts insects, which then disperse the spores so more stinkhorns may be hatched, proving Nature does have a sense of humor.

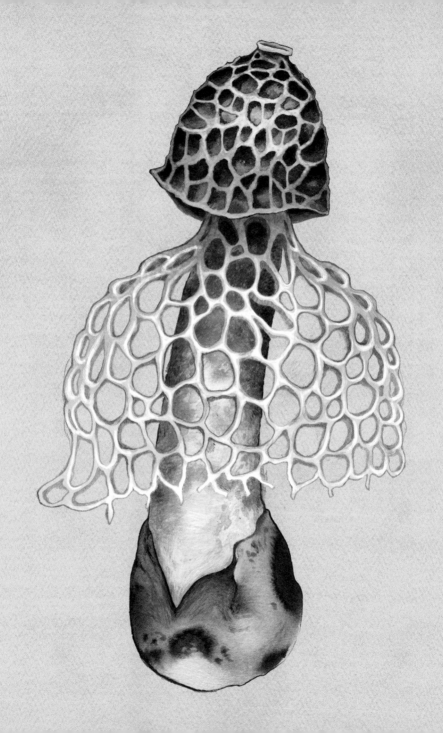

Phallus indusiatus

Bridal Veil Stinkhorn

EDIBILITY ⁘ Yes (rare), unlike others belonging to the *Phallus* genus that may only be edible in the egg stage; others are poisonous, so always triple-check identification if it's your intention to eat this.

MANIFESTING INFLUENCE ⁘ Attraction, fertility, intuition, romance, seeing through deception.

OTHER COMMON NAMES ⁘ Bamboo mushroom, basket stinkhorn, bridal veil, crinoline stinkhorn, veiled lady.

T HIS FAIRLY large member (up to 10 inches, or 25 centimeters, tall) of the *Phallus* genus is rather demure looking, veiled in lacy netting and reminiscent of a blushing bride. That's about as far as the demure personality goes, for like all stinkhorns, the bridal veil stinkhorn elicits love-it or hate-it sentiments and smells *strongly* of rotting flesh—mixed with mushrooms and garlic. The odor is a reproductive mechanism, attracting carrion flies to help spread its spores and create more forest brides. The mushroom grows worldwide in tropical regions and has long been used for its antibacterial properties. A rare delicacy, in China the bridal veil stinkhorn was collected to be served on special occasions, gracing such illustrious tables as that of the Qing dynasty's Empress Dowager Cixi when served as part of her sixtieth birthday celebration. It is still cultivated in China for its ability to lower blood pressure and other ailments, and for its use in fine dining and home cooking.

There are a number of look-alikes, even some with colored skirts. If you're lucky enough to meet this beauty, you won't soon forget her (and her aroma)!

Pleurotus ostreatus

Oyster Mushroom

EDIBILITY ❖ Edible; the younger, smaller mushrooms are better, and considered a delicacy in many Asian cuisines. They have a mild licorice aroma and meaty texture.

MANIFESTING INFLUENCE ❖ Abundance, attraction, consistency, protection from the unknown, recovery, transformation.

OTHER COMMON NAMES ❖ Hiratake, oyster fungus.

WHETHER FOUND on decaying and dead hardwood in the "wild," or grown commercially and foraged from the grocery store, the oyster mushroom possesses some superhero qualities.

Oyster mushrooms can be found in their natural habitat year-round, in all seasons, but are particularly prolific in mild weather with sufficient rainfall. The "oyster" in the name comes from the graceful fan-shaped mushroom cap's resemblance to an oyster shell, and it has an odd habit of growing its stem, if there is one, a bit sideways from the cap. As a result, these mushrooms usually grow horizontally on the wood, frequently in impressive clusters. Though typically of light-colored hues of caramel and tan, oyster mushrooms can be found in a range of colors, including pink.

Their fantastic ability to metabolize is proving remarkable for mycoremediation (see page 77) applications, particularly in oil-spill cleanup and removing heavy metals and other contaminants from soil.

In traditional Chinese medicine, the oyster mushroom is a medicinal mushroom and has been used to control high blood pressure. In more recent studies, oyster mushrooms have been shown to stop the growth of specific cancer cells, such as in breast and colon cancers. Oyster mushrooms also naturally produce statins, useful in lowering cholesterol.

Pink Waxcap

EDIBILITY ⁘ Edible, but threatened; rare to find and recommended to leave, respectfully, in place when found.

MANIFESTING INFLUENCE ⁘ Compassion, forgiveness, friendship, grace.

OTHER COMMON NAMES ⁘ Ballerina waxcap, pink ballerina, pink meadow cap.

THIS DELICATE pastel-pink dancer graces Europe's and especially the United Kingdom's natural fields and grasslands (and churchyards!) from late summer through fall, which have been seeing a decline over the recent decades. As an unfortunate consequence, its survival is threatened due to loss of its natural habitat. It is on the Red List in many places, meaning it is given legal protection from being disturbed in its natural habitat. Other similar species have been recorded in the United States and a few other places but are not believed to be related.

Its name is derived from the distinct, cone-shaped, pink waxy cap it sports, which then flattens and splits as it ages, forming a flouncy layered tutu supported by its slender pale-pink stalk. And, as all accomplished ballerinas have close and beneficial relationships with their dance partners, the pink waxcap thrives in symbiosis with mosses. It is one of the most beautiful waxcaps, and the only waxcap with a pointy cap. This elegant jewel is a special sighting and evokes the possibility of a fairy corps de ballet nearby. Savor the performance; let it fill you with joy.

Psilocybe semilanceata

Liberty Cap

EDIBILITY ❖ Hallucinogenic; treat as poisonous.

MANIFESTING INFLUENCE ❖ Freedom, grounding, intuition.

OTHER COMMON NAMES ❖ Magic mushroom, shroom, Welsh tea.

THIS UNASSUMING little brown mushroom (LBM) has a weighty name descended from history. The liberty cap, or Phrygian cap, was historically an actual cap given to and worn by freed enslaved peoples of the Roman Republic. It became the symbol of Roman freedom upon the murder of Julius Caesar and it reached its height of popularity when picked up and worn as the *bonnet rouge*, the symbolic red cap of the French Revolution's supporters, then upon its adoption by American revolutionary groups to communicate their revolt against British rule, hoisted high upon a liberty pole in town squares as a defiant display of freedom. The lore of the liberty cap morphed into an association with a mere little fairy cap mushroom that needed a name and that bore a remarkable resemblance to the famous hat.

It was decades later that its potent mind-freeing properties, in the form of the psychoactive compound called psilocybin, were discovered, becoming a well-known symbol of psychedelic counterculture and self-discovery. Today liberty cap grows with independent abandon from summer through fall in wet grasslands of the United Kingdom, Northern Europe, and the United States and Canada.

Although "magic" mushrooms have been used in religious ceremonies and for medicinal purposes by various cultures for many thousands of years, they are still illegal in many places, but their legal status is undergoing change. That said, if you don't want your freedom impinged upon, stay away from illegal substances, including liberty cap mushrooms.

Rhodotus palmatus

Wrinkled Peach

EDIBILITY ❖ Inedible.

MANIFESTING INFLUENCE ❖ Changing luck, creativity, joy.

OTHER COMMON NAMES ❖ Apricot fungus, netted *Rhodotus*, rosy vein cap.

T HIS RARE, stunning mushroom feeds off felled hardwoods, especially freshly felled elm trees, and so the devastation caused by Dutch elm disease, which provided an initial feeding ground for this mushroom, eventually wiped out much of its habitat in parts of the world, putting it on the endangered Red List in about a dozen European countries. When it is found, it's typically in summer through fall in the United Kingdom, parts of Europe and Asia, and North America.

The mushroom was first described in 1785 by French naturalist Jean Baptiste François (Pierre) Bulliard. It was later moved to another category by another botanist, and currently, because of its beautifully unique characteristics, is the only species in its genus. Its name *palmatus* is thought to have been inspired by the webbing's resemblance to the lines in a person's palm, though it really rather looks more brain-like. The dramatic web of ridges, wrinkles, and veins, a distinctive feature, on the slimy, rubbery cap develops during alternating periods of wet and dry weather. Consistently wet weather puffs up the cap like a puffball (page 135). Its coloration, usually bubble-gum pink to peachy to salmon-colored, can vary widely and has been found to be a result of the spectrum of light reaching the forest floor. The delicate pink gills under the peach-colored cap are almost mesmerizing to look at. For unknown reasons, the mushroom sometimes "bleeds" or oozes a pinkish-red to orangish-red liquid. Though rare, this tiny beauty can be found from time to time and is cause for celebration and a moment of gratitude for the wonder that is Nature.

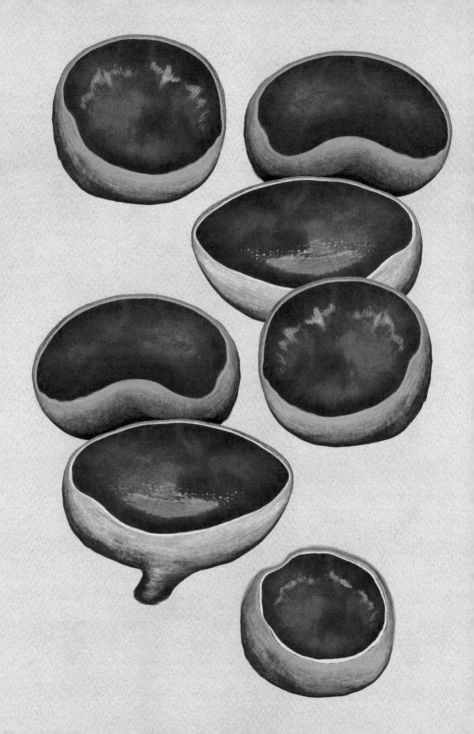

Sarcoscypha austriaca

Scarlet Elf Cup

EDIBILITY ❖ Debated, but commonly agreed it's not.

MANIFESTING INFLUENCE ❖ Connections, love, optimism, rebirth, vitality.

OTHER COMMON NAMES ❖ Fairies' bath, moss cup, red cup, scarlet elf cap.

A CHEERY SPOT of color smiling among the forest-floor debris, the scarlet elf cup is a welcome sighting—akin to a kiss from the fairies. These scarlet- to orange-hued cup-shaped mushrooms are a magical departure from the solemn earth-toned relatives typically found among the dark, dank leaves and decaying wood, appearing from early winter to early spring over much of the Northern Hemisphere when the world needs a pop of life. Their red color partly comes from beta-carotene. Though not edible, the Oneida people were known to use the scarlet elf cup medicinally, dried and ground to a powder, to staunch bleeding.

They emit a slight audible "poof" when releasing their spores (though you must listen closely). Their forest job is to help recycle dead wood into nutrients to support the Earth, and their utilitarian bowl shape is said to be the perfect spot for the woodland elves to gather for a bit of forest gossip and to drink the morning dew, or a delightful respite for a soothing fairy bath after a long day of spreading fairy dust. When you happen upon this jewel of the forest, stop a moment to be grateful for the magic.

Sarcosoma globosum

Witches' Cauldron

EDIBILITY ❖ Unknown, but highly unlikely and discouraged.

MANIFESTING INFLUENCE ❖ Grounding, manifesting hopes and dreams, transformation.

OTHER COMMON NAMES ❖ Charred-pancake cup.

S TUMBLING UPON the spooky witches' cauldron may have you looking nearby for signs of the coven that abandoned it! (And, it is a rarity, so be grateful for your good fortune.) If you are to find one, it will likely be in a northern climate, particularly Northern Europe—typically in established old-growth forests—or northern regions of North America, especially the Great Lakes Region. Sprouting from the forest floor once spring's thaw increases the availability of water, this large, dark-brown, cup-shaped fungus really does look like a cauldron (one that might be owned by a witch, or not!), hence its name, incubating some sort of gelatinous stew comprising the decomposing matter on which it thrives.

First described in 1793, it is now considered rare and has been labeled as threatened, mainly due to the toil and trouble brought about by changes in land management that affect its habitat, including changes to the logging industry and the cessation of cattle grazing in forests, which cleared the way for the mushrooms' happy growth.

Its dark colors of brown and black speak of protection, grounding, and strength, and temper the fear you may feel on discovering it. Decomposing forest litter is its main job, though other details about it are scarce. Its rarity and overall witchy vibe, though, are mysterious enough to get the mind churning as to its larger role in the forest kingdom. If you are lucky enough to spot one, listen closely to determine whether it will give up its secrets.

Suillus luteus

Slippery Jack

EDIBILITY ⁙ Yes, when thoroughly cooked and the slimy coating is peeled, but with the possibility of stomach upset in exchange for not much taste or aroma.

MANIFESTING INFLUENCE ⁙ Abundance, cooperation, grounding, stability.

OTHER COMMON NAMES ⁙ Pine boletus, sticky bun.

THIS MUSHROOM, geographically widespread across the Northern Hemisphere, fruits abundantly (it's said that bushels can be harvested from a single row of pine trees) from summer to fall, typically in symbiosis with pine and spruce trees. It gets its somewhat silly common name from the fact that its cap is super slimy and slippery when wet—watch your step! (It's not known who "Jack" is—maybe the person who named it?)

First described in 1753 by Carl Linnaeus, it is classified among the boletes, featuring tubes extending from beneath the cap rather than gills. As the mushroom ages, a white veil forms a distinctive white ring that changes to shades of purple just beneath the muddy-colored cap that covers the lemon-colored pores (tubes). The stalk is very distinct: light-colored, with tiny brown dots at the top, sticky, slimy brown in the middle, and purplish mottled brown at the bottom.

Though deemed edible, not all agree on the appeal of its spongy texture and mild flavor, except in the Slavic cultures, where the mushroom-obsessed regard it as a delicacy!

This mushroom is very deceiving as to the depths of its personality. Look beneath the slimy surface and you'll discover all its unique colorings and characteristics, perhaps offering us a lesson in avoiding judgment of those you don't know well.

Though slippery in name (*Suillus* actually derives from a Latin word meaning "pig"!), you'll feel the supremely stabilizing and grounding energies emanating from this forest friend.

Trametes versicolor,
Coriolus versicolor

Turkey Tail

EDIBILITY ⁙ Edible, but tough; often used to make tea.

MANIFESTING INFLUENCE ⁙ Attraction, good health, new life, transformation.

OTHER COMMON NAMES ⁙ Kawaratake (Japanese name),
yun zhi (in Chinese medicine).

THE TURKEY TAIL mushroom, so-named for its splendid resemblance to the tom turkey's colorful, full-on showstopping tail—so colorful and long-lived, in fact, the mushroom was once used to decorate both tables and hats, and even made into jewelry—is a stunner. The turkey tail is valued worldwide for its healing, medicinal properties. It is abundant, growing year-round in clusters, or bracts, and can usually be spotted wherever there is decaying hardwood, such as dead branches or tree stumps. Known anecdotally to stimulate the immune system and fight cancer, as well as to have an affinity for supporting healthy kidney function, it is used and studied as an alternative medicine in many countries and has been used historically in traditional Chinese medicine to cure many ailments, including infections and inflammation, for over one thousand years.

In a study including the United States Department of Defense, the turkey tail mushroom, an efficient composter, was one of only two found to be able to consume a potent neurotoxin, one used in the Iran-Iraq War, as its primary source of nutrients, thereby neutralizing its threat. The National Institutes of Health have demonstrated turkey tail's ability to reduce the size of cancerous tumors and increase the effectiveness of chemotherapy. With much ongoing research happening, its true "tale" of benefits is likely yet uncovered.

Tremella mesenterica

Witch's Butter

EDIBILITY ⁘ Though no agreement on this exists, it is not poisonous and many say it is edible for texture because it is flavorless.

MANIFESTING INFLUENCE ⁘ Manifesting, optimism, rejuvenation.

OTHER COMMON NAMES ⁘ Golden jelly fungus, yellow brain fungus.

L OOKING LIKE softened butter, when found oozing at the entrance of your home or smeared upon your gate, it's a sure sign you've been put under a witch's spell. Destroying this mushroom—sticking it with pins is the prescription for draining the mushroom and releasing the spell—is said to cause harm to the witch herself, or cause her to appear!

Found worldwide, year-round, but mainly seen in winter, this bright-yellow jelly fungus is most noticeable for its color; its size ranges only from ½ to 1½ inches (1 to 3.8 centimeters), growing in squishy, rubbery, wavy blobs clumped together on dead hardwoods in cooler months after heavy rains. Though found growing on dead wood, this fungus doesn't actually feed off the wood, but rather another fungus underneath it called a crust fungus (genus *Peniophora*) that is feeding off the wood. It deflates and hardens when the weather dries, but is rejuvenated with the next rain (which may debunk the draining theory of killing it).

Witch's butter has a history of use in traditional Chinese medicine as an expectorant, and as a thickener in some Chinese recipes, like soup. Current research on this mushroom focuses on stimulating the immune system and preventing cancer.

If spied on your doorway, you may want to walk in a circle, counter-clockwise, three times to dispel the negative energy . . . just in case.

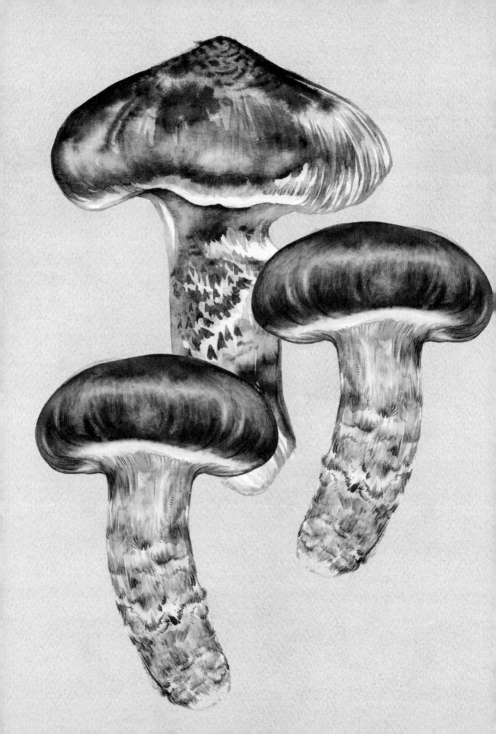

Matsutake

EDIBILITY ⁂ Highly sought after; has a thick, white flesh with an earthy, spicy flavor often described as an acquired taste, and often an intense woodsy foliage aroma, which some describe as like cinnamon.

MANIFESTING INFLUENCE ⁂ Health, longevity, luxury, relationships.

OTHER COMMON NAMES ⁂ Brown matsutake, white matsutake.

FROM FALL through winter, mushroom foragers seek the elusive matsutake. Possibly the world's most expensive and one of its most highly prized edible mushrooms, *matsutake* means "pine mushroom" in Japanese, where it originates, and is so named for the pine forests in which it grows wild in Japan, China, and Korea. Due to loss of habitat, however, matsutake is becoming endangered in Japan and other places in the world. Two related species, *Tricholoma magnivelare* and *Tricholoma murrillianum*, grow in the western United States and Europe and are also referred to and sold as matsutake. Because of their rarity and inability to be cultivated due to their unique symbiotic relationships developed in their natural habitat, matsutakes can be quite expensive.

Matsutakes are particularly highly prized in Japan, on a par with or even more so than truffles, and are considered a luxury item, often given as gifts symbolizing fertility, good fortune, and happiness—and even finding themselves the subject of rhapsodic poetry. It is the subject of anime and the symbol of fall festivals. When used in cooking, it must be fresh and the matsutake is used sparingly as the flavor is so intense and the mushroom is so prized. In Japanese culture, as other mushrooms are, the matsutake is considered a medicinal food, one thought to ensure good health and a long life. It also shows promise as an anticancer agent.

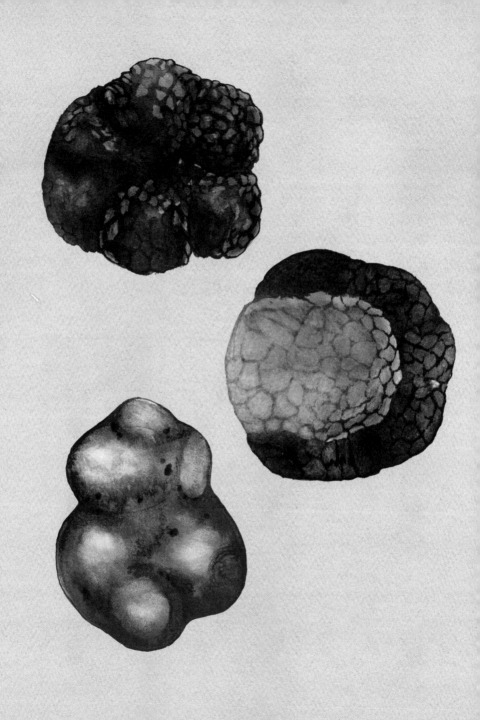

Tuber melanosporum (French Périgord black truffle),
Tuber magnatum (Piedmont white truffle)

Truffle

EDIBILITY ⫶ An edible delicacy!

MANIFESTING INFLUENCE ⫶ Devotion, intuition, love, wealth.

OTHER COMMON NAMES ⫶ Depending on location, descriptive.

A MEMBER OF the ascomycete family of fungi, the first recorded mention of truffles dates back to the 1700s BCE and the Sumerians. Later, Pliny the Elder tells us ancient Romans adored this fungus, who copied its use in the kitchen from the Etruscans, often saving the mushrooms for their most important guests—along with other exotic delicacies, like peacock brains.

One of the earliest known cookbooks thought to have been written in Rome during the first century CE, *Apicius: De Re Coquinaria*, contains an entire chapter on truffles that includes seven ways to prepare them, though best results are implied when they're prepared by a master chef.

The Romans and ancient Greeks believed this luxury arose where a lightning bolt hurled to Earth by Jupiter (Zeus) struck and so, because of his reputation for sexual prowess, was also deemed an aphrodisiac and food of the gods. The English poet Lord Byron reputedly displayed one on his desk, kept there for its aromatic inspiration. And, because of its slightly mysterious origins and the superstitions rampant during the Middle Ages, the truffle became associated with witches, called witch's fare. The Catholic Church called its fascinating fragrances the work of the Devil, and therefore something to be avoided at all costs.

Dubbed the "black diamond of cuisine" by famed epicure Brillat-Savarin, the much-loved though hard-to-find truffle may just be the world's most expensive food, compounded by the fact that it fades and spoils just days after harvest. France, Italy, and Spain are the three principal countries producing truffles, yet not one of the three recognizes the others' as serious. That said, this knobby-looking, irregularly shaped sphere can sell for upwards of $450 per pound (0.45 kilogram), with its value being determined based on size and aroma: pungent, earthy, and a bit funky. And white truffles, being rarer than the black variety, have seen prices as high as $4,500 per pound. The most expensive single truffle ever sold to date, though not the largest, was a 2.86-pound (1.3 kilograms) black truffle from Croatia for $330,000!

This rare and revered delicacy of the food world is most closely associated with Europe, particularly France (where it was served at the wedding banquet of Charles VI and Isabeau of Bavaria in 1385!) and Italy, but also grows in Africa, Asia, and North America. Truffles grow in a symbiotic association with specific hardwood trees, such as the oak, and some conifers, as the source of their energy needs—and in quite finicky conditions. Unlike other mushrooms, their fruiting body grows entirely underground, with no aboveground stem or cap to make them easier to spot with the naked eye. This subterranean adaptation is thought to have evolved to protect the mushroom from harsh environmental conditions.

And as they exhibit no visible features by which to spot them, ethical and sustainable harvesting (technically, hunting) of the elusive truffle is done by dogs trained specifically to detect their mature aroma, which ensures they'll be flavorful, and indicates their location, which tends to be a highly guarded secret. The mouthwatering aroma is also the mechanism by which they reproduce . . . attracting other animals to eat them as food and then, well, pass on their spores in other areas to grow. Female pigs, too, have been used to find truffles—without any training—as the truffles' scent mimics the male pig's sex hormone, to which the females are attracted naturally. However, they tend to get so excited that they eat what they find, and wreak havoc on the ecosystem in the process! Humans, alas, can only detect the glorious smell once the truffle has been cut. Historically considered an aphrodisiac, pigs are not the only ones excited to devour the tantalizing truffle!

TRUFFLE TRIVIA

Being one of the most sought-after, talked-about, significantly scented, and highly priced fungi in the world can lead to a number of interesting facts and lore. Here are some of truffle's most tantalizing...

* Aphrodite, the Greek goddess of love, loved truffles.

* Greek philosopher Plutarch believed truffles were actually mud cooked by lightning.

* Truffles were deemed harmful by the medieval theory of the humors, which declared all foods grown underground to be undesirable and potentially harmful, and so were left only for the peasants to consume.

* King Louis XIV adored the truffle and is credited with reviving its reputation and popularity as part of France's elevated cuisine.

* After the World Wars, most of the truffle's natural habitat was destroyed and had to be recultivated to revive this delicacy.

* Some people are genetically disposed to dislike truffles, particularly the smell, which they say is more akin to dirty socks than an aphrodisiac.

* In Italy, you must pass an exam to become licensed to be a truffle hunter, and hunting truffles without a dog is forbidden (random and numerous holes dug without any clue to the truffles' location is damaging to the environment).

* Today, the adorable Lagotto Romagnolo is the preferred breed of truffle-hunting dog.

* Chocolate "truffles" are coated in cocoa powder to mimic the look and feel of the soil.

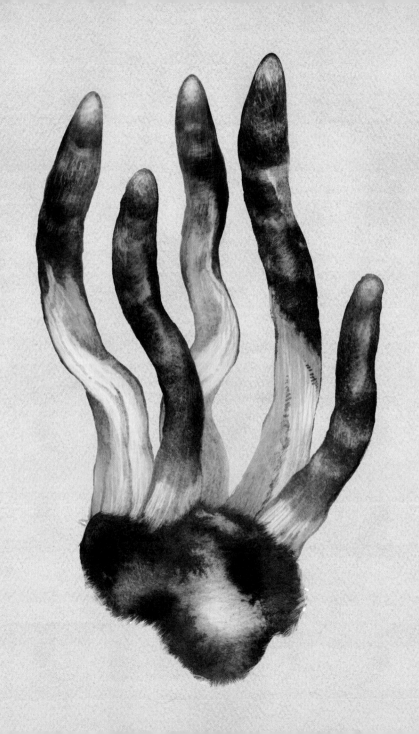

Xylaria polymorpha

Dead Man's Fingers

EDIBILITY ✣ Inedible.

MANIFESTING INFLUENCE ✣ Enrichment, support in grief.

OTHER COMMON NAMES ✣ None.

Corpse-like, blackened, wrinkled, knobby fingers push up from the ground as if to claw their way out of the grave, reaching, pleading for help... Meet dead man's fingers, a spooktacular spectacle seen "returning from the dead" in parts of North America and all over the United Kingdom and Ireland, as well as Europe. Depending on when you spot this gruesome specimen, you may see variations in its appearance. When young, for instance, the "fingers" are a deathly pale bluish-gray with whitish tips, or nails, all blackening as they age.

For its part in the circle of life, dead man's fingers help break down decaying wood and, in the process, enrich that soil with nutrients that nourish the many invertebrates that dwell there. It is usually found growing in three- to six-finger clumps at the base of dead beechwood. Though not impressive in size (it's typically 1½ to 3 inches, or 3 to 7.5 centimeters, in height), dead man's fingers definitely bring the creep factor. This mushroom has a long life cycle throughout most of the year, and so can be found nearly year-round. If you happen to spot it while walking along in the forest, a friendly wave and a smile are all that are required as you keep... on... walking...

Basket Fungus

Manifesting with Mushrooms

MANIFESTING, THOUGH SEEMINGLY A LITTLE MYSTERIOUS, is simply the process of bringing about change and desired outcomes in life through our focused beliefs and actions. And as all action springs from intention, all intentions should be born of the seeds of gratitude.

If you're so inclined, manifesting your best life, combining intention, action, and affirmation, is a powerful potion to add to mushrooms' symbolic and inherent energy. That energy and its inspiration to help manifest your dreams and desires come from the mushroom's color, shape, scent, constitution, texture, habitat, environment, symbiotic or other relationships, growth pattern, history, lore, chemical makeup, and personal intuition. Working

Intuition is our innate ability to tune in to the vibrations around us and sense their connections in our world. Many refer to intuition as their "gut," and learning to hear and trust your gut are important skills. You'll not only gain insights into the world around you, but you will also sense when your magic is working, or perhaps needs a boost. In addition, if your gut is warning you something is not right, take heed. It's usually right. Your intuition is the best tool in your magical bag.

in harmony with Nature to live a purposeful life also promotes peace, tolerance, balance, and the intention to honor Earth for her gifts. There is no right or wrong, only what speaks to you and empowers you to be your best self.

With a little work and some focused thought, there's no limit to what you can achieve. If you've never thought about it before, there's not much to lose, and lots to be gained, by giving it a try.

Intentions

The law of vibration is the foundation of the law of attraction and tells us every "thing" vibrates. As everything is made differently, it vibrates at different frequencies. So, too, do your intentions. Some frequencies are obvious, like color or music, but some are not. This universal energy means all things are interconnected and influenced by each other, and like ripples in a pond or mushrooms in a fairy ring, they expand outward. Formulating your energy-filled intentions and releasing them into the Universe allows the energy to influence the results you desire and come back to you in abundance. It's the idea that like attracts like.

Manifesting with Nature's magic to live your best magical life depends on setting intentions with the natural rhythms surrounding you: to know deep in your heart what you want or need, or what needs attention in your life, understand why you want or need it, and commit to making it happen. Reaching deep into your soul to acknowledge, without fear or judgment, what is important to you and what will make you truly happy are the next steps. Defining intentions keeps us focused and living in the present, or mindfully, staying true to our values and dreams, and can help improve our overall sense of well-being.

Dedicating time to this process lets us slow down and revel in the quiet to hear what our hearts are saying, which can inspire new ideas to take root. Taking inspiration from the splendid mushroom, we know those roots run deep and wide, nourish the system, and sprout when the time is right. Magic happens when you need it most, not necessarily when you want it.

As you wander this path of manifesting with Nature, take time to be present in the moment. Set goals and intentions based on your beliefs, hopes, and desires. Draw the magic to you or send a blessing into the world—but do no harm. And remember, mushrooms are living, breathing beings that deserve our care and respect, for they have much to teach us. They can also be harmful if not used properly. Never ingest anything without proper knowledge of what you have and never do anything that feels intuitively wrong. May you receive many blessings in return.

CHECK YOUR ENERGY

Although all things vibrate with energy, all energy is not the same. A higher vibrational energy—one attuned to the good, the positive, the higher calling of the Universe—is what we're aiming for in our manifesting work. It is when energies are high, filled with intent, and then released into the Universe that the magic really starts.

When energy is low, you feel off-kilter, maybe from illness or anger or jealousy or grief, things that can block the free flow of energy and keep it in a negative state.

To begin your manifesting work, you may want to assess your personal energy level. If it's in a negative state, there are some things you can do to boost it into the positive realm of peace, gratitude, grounding, and joy before you begin.

* **CLEANSE AWAY NEGATIVITY OR THE BLUES.** Open the windows, sweep your space with fresh sage branches, or perform a smoke cleanse, focusing on corners and closets where stagnant energy lurks. Visualize the bad vibes being chased away, or do an emotional sweep—pause and feel gratitude for all that is good. Breathe in the fresh energy while visualizing yourself releasing any anger, hurt, fear, or negativity.

* **SET AN INTENTION FOR JOY.** Sometimes simply recognizing the low energy state and committing to change it are all that's needed. Then, act joyful: sing, dance, volunteer, do something for others, create in any way that allows you to express your joy.

* **DECIDE WHAT REALLY MAKES YOU HAPPY.** Be honest, nonjudgmental, accepting, and realistic in your assessment. You cannot raise your vibrational energy if your actions are in constant misalignment with your heart.

* **BE KIND TO YOURSELF.** Accept who you are. Talk to yourself as you would your best friend. Engage in meditation (see page 59), or explore other self-care rituals that make you feel your best. Forgive yourself and others.

* **ENGAGE WITH NATURE.** Take a walk in the forest and spend time listening to the mushrooms' musings!

TIPS FOR MUSHROOM MANIFESTING SUCCESS

* Be respectful, sustainable, and intentional in your mushroom selection, harvesting, and use. Honor the mushrooms and use them with gratitude for the energies offered.

* Be respectful of our Earth and all her inhabitants.

* Be respectful of your intuition; let it guide your manifesting practice and relationship with the Universe.

* Practice patience along with gratitude.

* Work with the seasons to honor Nature's pace—perfection can't be hurried.

* Start magic with intention—and never to do harm.

* Believe. Understand the power you have when you combine intention with words, actions, and mushrooms' innate energy.

CAUTION!

Mushrooms can be poisonous, definitely not the magical quality we're going for here. When in doubt, never handle, eat, or use anything you're not 300 percent sure is safe—even then, use caution. There are hundreds of mushroom-related paraphernalia that can inspire instead and represent the magic within.

- ✳ Books about mushrooms

- ✳ Brew a mug of mushroom coffee or try another functional mushroom beverage from a reputable retailer

- ✳ Candy mushrooms

- ✳ Crochet some mushrooms

- ✳ Cut your food into the shape of a mushroom

- ✳ Footstools

- ✳ Garden decorations

- ✳ Grow your own mushrooms with a grow kit

- ✳ Keep track of your intentions and the work you're doing in a journal decorated with images of mushrooms

- ✳ Listen to some mushroom music (see page 46)

- ✳ Make a mushroom fragrance your signature manifesting scent!

* Mushroom lamps and night-lights

* Mushroom photos, prints, and drawings

* Mushroom pillows

* Mushroom sculptures and mobiles

* Mushroom-shaped crystals

* Mushroom-shaped glasses to drink a toast to your intentions

* Mushroom-shaped incense holders

* Mushroom-shaped or scented candles and mushroom-shaped candleholders

* Mushroom socks, or a scarf, or a T-shirt

* Mushroom-themed tarot cards

* Season your food with intention using mushroom-shaped salt and pepper shakers

* Skin care products containing mushroom extracts (see page 69)

* Toy mushrooms

All these, and more (the list is virtually unending, like mushroom species themselves!), can be physical stand-ins on which to focus your intentions and energies. Your magic will be no less effective and a lot more fun.

Using Color to Manifest Magic

Turning to Nature's offerings gives you access to an infinite rainbow of colors to work with, built in to naturally boost energy and influence outcomes. And yes, mushrooms *do* come in all colors of the rainbow! In addition to a mushroom's shape, scent, habitat, and other characteristics, color can indicate innate magical power and help direct how best to work with it.

Each color represents a different energy level/frequency/vibration, and frequencies affect us variously—and individually. Following are colors and their meanings based on energy characteristics to help you tap into mushroom wisdom and their magical messages. Because colors are frequently assigned different or multiple meanings, and we all have our own memories and associations with color throughout life, experiment, have fun, and stay in tune with your intuition. Use the colors that feel right or speak to you.

BLACK: Powerful healing, protection, security, support in grief.

BLUE: Calm, healing, health, kindness, meditation, patience, sincerity, tranquility.

BRIGHT ORANGE: Happiness.

BRIGHT PINK: Creativity, glamour.

BRONZE/BROWN: Common sense, experience, feeling grounded, longevity, prosperity, stability, strength.

DARK BLUE: Peace, tranquility.

GOLD: Attraction, changing luck, creativity, elegance, energy, fertility, joy, prestige, prosperity, success.

GREEN: Abundance, feeling grounded, fertility, friendship, good luck, growth, healing, renewal, success.

LAVENDER: Intuition, peace, protection, spiritual growth.

ORANGE: Ambition, attraction, building energy, changing luck, courage, creativity, emotional healing, health, individuality, joy, warmth.

PINK: Calm, clairvoyance, compassion, faith, forgiveness, friendship, harmony, joy, tenderness.

PURPLE: Authority, intuition, prosperity, spiritual awareness, stress reduction, success, wealth, wisdom.

RED/DEEP RED: Courage, passion, power, protection, romantic love, security, vitality.

SILVER/GRAY: Clairvoyance, cleansing, healing, moonlight, peace, rest, truth.

TURQUOISE: Awakening, awareness, enlightenment.

VIOLET: Creativity, dreams, healing intuition, psychic powers.

WHITE: Clairvoyance, cleansing, peace, protection, security, truth.

YELLOW: Communication, confidence, creativity, happiness, intuition, mental clarity, optimism, personal power and self-esteem, success in business, warmth.

DAILY & PLANETARY CORRESPONDENCES, COLOR & MANIFESTING

As the days of the week are named for the seven classical planets (the five planets visible to the naked eye plus the Sun and Moon) and so carry a related energetic correspondence, crafting a spell, ritual, or prayer on a particular day triples the energetic influence of the mushroom you've selected for manifesting:

DAILY INFLUENCE + PLANETARY INFLUENCE + MUSHROOM ENERGY

Boost the benefit of daily correspondences further by incorporating color (see page 188). Each day and its planetary namesake have corresponding colors that are particularly strong when used together to increase your influence on the outcomes you seek. You may find your intuition or observations provide a different perspective. Follow what makes you comfortable and resonates with your heart and intentions.

AS ABOVE, SO BELOW. AS WITHIN, SO WITHOUT.

SUNDAY *(for the Sun)*
COLORS: GOLD, LAVENDER, ORANGE, YELLOW

When working your magic on Sunday, take advantage of its solar energies related to changing luck, confidence, creativity, energy, growth, healing, hope, intuition, joy, male health, mental clarity, peace, personal power and self-esteem, prosperity, protection, spirituality, strength, success, and wealth.

MONDAY *(for the Moon)*
COLORS: GRAY, LAVENDER, SILVER, WHITE

Monday's lunar tendencies call forth clairvoyance, cleansing, emotional healing, family, fertility, flexibility, guidance, inner goddess wisdom, intuition, peace, prophetic dreams, truth, and rejuvenation.

Note that because of mushrooms' particularly watery nature, in general, the energies of the Moon, associated with the fluid waters of emotion and its magnetic effect on the tides, are especially attuned to manifesting with mushrooms.

TUESDAY *(for Mars)*

COLORS: BLACK, DEEP RED/RED

Honor your inner warrior and channel Mars's energy when you seek bravery, courage, energy, love, passion, patience, power, and protection.

WEDNESDAY *(for Mercury)*

COLORS: ORANGE, PURPLE

Send your manifesting energies into the Universe on the wings of Mercury for charisma, communication, creativity, knowledge, spiritual awareness, and wisdom.

THURSDAY *(for Jupiter)*

COLORS: BLUE/ROYAL BLUE, GREEN, LAVENDER, PURPLE

The sky's the limit with Jupiter on your side. His nurturing power can boost your manifesting energies when casting for career, faith, generosity of goods and spirit, growth, judgment, luck, patience, peace, sincerity, and wealth.

FRIDAY *(for Venus)*

COLORS: AQUA, GREEN, LAVENDER, PINK, ROSE

Born from the sea and destined to love both gods and mortals, Venus can help you attract abundance, affection, beauty, fertility, forgiveness, friendship, good luck, harmony, love, money, peace, pleasure, renewal, romance, sexuality, and success.

SATURDAY *(for Saturn)*

COLORS: BLACK, DEEP PURPLE, LAVENDER

With his deep connection to Earth as god of agriculture, Saturn's healing energies can guide you in matters of grounding and personal boundaries, home, justice, letting go, peace, and protection from negative energy.

Spells to Sprout Magic

Magic is hope and belief in our ability to influence outcomes with intention. Intentions well set are the spores that grow into our hopes, dreams, desires, and manifested outcomes of living a magical life. Those spores are microscopic: hard to see, easy to forget about, and difficult to imagine anything great arising from them. But that doesn't mean they're not there, nor does it mean they won't grow.

Magical living is the ability to see the wonder in all, feel the gratitude for what you have, and show up each day intending for it to be your best.

I offer here a few spells and ideas to incorporate the mysterious magical mushroom's energetic influence into everyday opportunities to manifest some magic.

May your magic sprout wings and transport you to your dreams. As above, so below.

BELIEVE IN YOUR MAGIC

If you're new to the idea of manifesting magic in your life, welcome. If you're fully on board, welcome back. To start, just step outside and look around at all the world has to offer, especially the natural world. Mother Nature creates her own kind of magic, of which mushrooms in all their glorious diversity and energy are just one type. Living with strength to believe in your magic gives you the gift of magic found in belief.

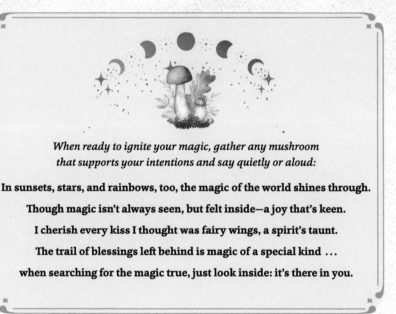

*When ready to ignite your magic, gather any mushroom
that supports your intentions and say quietly or aloud:*

In sunsets, stars, and rainbows, too, the magic of the world shines through.

Though magic isn't always seen, but felt inside—a joy that's keen.

I cherish every kiss I thought was fairy wings, a spirit's taunt.

The trail of blessings left behind is magic of a special kind ...

when searching for the magic true, just look inside: it's there in you.

PROTECTING PERSONAL BOUNDARIES

Being the life of the party has its benefits, but having others constantly crave your attention can be anything but life-giving. When it's time to set up—and protect—your personal boundaries for some me-time and recharging, take a cue from the stinkhorn (pages 151 and 153).

This attention-getter thrives, in its own way and in its own time, where it lands but definitely gives off that "do-not-disturb" vibe. Although you may wish to modulate your vibe so as not to scare people away, do stand firm in your desire to maintain your own company for a while.

With whatever representation of this charm you choose to work with, take some time to be clear about your intentions and feel the energy to grow in the space you need being transferred to you. If you'd like, cast a circle counterclockwise, around yourself, around an image of the stinkhorn, or in a ceremonial place outside among Nature, as a symbol of your boundaries to keep disturbances at bay.

When ready to commit, say quietly or aloud:

It's time for me, said thrice will be. The boundaries I have set must be.
For those who step beyond the line, invading space and time that's mine
beware the look that warns away, for here and now, you must not stay.
And if you turn to look away, that smell you smell is trust's decay.

INCREASING INTUITION

Your intuition is the well of wisdom that accumulates in your gut over a lifetime of experience. Whether you call it your third eye, trusting your gut, or having a hunch, we all have the gift of intuition—our innate ability to tune in to the vibrations around us and sense their connections in our world. It sees clearly, even when we don't, which is why we tend to second guess it. Some people are more aware of those vibrations than others, but anyone can learn to listen to and sense the unseen.

Whether trying to purposely boost your intuitive skills to further your manifesting influence or learning to listen more carefully when your gut is warning you, many mushrooms carry the energy of intuition. Amethyst deceiver (page 127), Caesar's mushroom (page 85), and liberty cap (page 159) are three good examples, as are the colors yellow and purple. When ready to open your mind and heart to the messages of the Universe, gather your representative mushrooms and sit quietly with them for a moment to clarify your intentions.

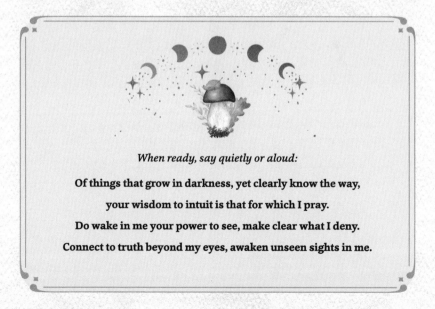

When ready, say quietly or aloud:

Of things that grow in darkness, yet clearly know the way,

your wisdom to intuit is that for which I pray.

Do wake in me your power to see, make clear what I deny.

Connect to truth beyond my eyes, awaken unseen sights in me.

YOU ARE PRICELESS!

To conjure a little love magic, look no further than the truffle (page 175). Not classically beautiful to look at, but tantalizing nonetheless, this lovely is adored for its uniqueness and treasured when found after playing a bit hard to get. When you want to be adored for the priceless treasure you are, let the truffle's aromatic energy to attract be your inspiration.

As fresh truffles tend to be expensive, you may want to seek out truffle oil, truffle paste, a jar of mushroom and truffle tapenade, canned truffles, truffle mayo, ketchup, or honey, or even truffle salt to work your magic. (Of course, use fresh truffles if you're lucky enough to have them!)

Mindfully incorporate your chosen truffle into your favorite appetizer, sauce, salad, or pasta dish as you define your intentions for manifesting love. If you have more of a sweet truffle tooth, choose a chocolate truffle for dessert. And, if you don't want to actually eat any truffles, burn a truffle-scented candle to add the element of fire so passions burn brighter.

When ready to be adored as only you deserve to be, take a sniff of truffle's exotic perfume, waft some into the air, and say quietly or aloud:

Aromas do intoxicate and truffle's never fails. It speaks of inner beauty and an earthiness that's rare.

I call on truffle's magic, for indeed that's what it is, to lead my true love to my door, no words need to be said.

When magic sparks ignite the flame that passion needs to burn, true love that's worth the price it bears is one that will endure.

SECOND CHANCES

Everyone deserves a second chance, and the charming fairy ring mushroom (page 137) may be just the ally you need when it's your turn—to give or receive. From the most serious of harms to the simplest misunderstanding or negative first impression, countless situations can cause us to reject or be rejected by others. Open your heart to forgiveness, and being forgiven, for a boost of happiness and emotional well-being. Second chances are never automatic, though, so trust your intuition if it does not feel right.

Like the gentle rain that will rehydrate and "resurrect" the fairy ring mushroom to a productive second (and more) life, imagine a gentle cleansing rain falling on you . . . let it wash away any self-hatred or hatred of others and "resurrect" your heart's ability to forgive.

When truly ready, say quietly or aloud:

**A second chance is like the rain, to cleanse
the soul and heal the pain.**

The choice is mine, it must be so, for to forgive is to let go.

**For "chance" is luck and luck is fate: I vow this
chance won't go to waste.**

FEELING CONNECTED

When you need to feel part of the whole, physically and spiritually, find inspiration from lion's mane (page 121). This mushroom's fierce presence belies the microscopic spore that was its humble beginning. And its quiet fortitude masks its great potential.

Choose something white, for clarity, truth, and protection, and to help connect to your crown chakra and the universal purpose you wish to join. This energy center controls thought, wisdom, enlightenment, and self-knowledge. When balanced, you feel beautiful and connected to everything and everyone; when unbalanced, you may experience confusion, a lack of focus, and a lack of connection to the things around you—you look for happiness outside versus in.

When you're ready to see your small but mighty part in this journey and feel connected with its outcome, visualize the fierce face that is lion's mane, ground yourself with a few calming breaths, and imagine your crown chakra, at the top of your head, radiating a glowing white light of illumination.

When ready to continue, say quietly or aloud:

The light within is mine to share. To keep it dark creates despair.

I breathe the light for all to see, to recognize the harmony.

I seek the light, for in its glow, the world above is so below.

Though small my part is in this song, my voice is heard and I am strong.

Each note connects the timeless tune, to keep us whole and heal our wounds.

LETTING GO

As the first to stir from the sleepy forest floor in spring, morels (page 141) are a sign of new growth and opportunity. Sometimes, to encourage or make room for that growth, something must be pruned or let go. Taking inspiration from the tradition of setting fire to wooded areas—to burn away one thing to make way for another (in this case a lush growth of morels in spring) to thrive—this short ritual can help you do just that.

The beauty of releasing something that no longer serves, or holds us back, is in the freedom it provides—from guilt, from worry, from fear, from disappointment. In its place is a wide-open space ready to be filled with intentions that align with our priorities and actions that take us in a new, positive direction.

Gather a pen, piece of paper, cauldron, matches, and water (just in case). On the paper, write down the thing or things holding you back or getting in your way of true success. They may have at one time served you well, but no longer feed your soul.

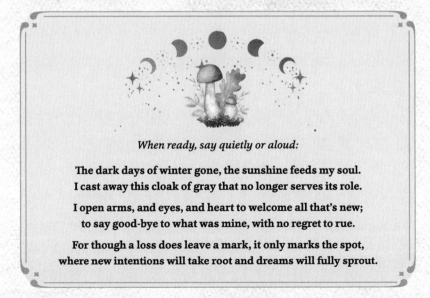

When ready, say quietly or aloud:

The dark days of winter gone, the sunshine feeds my soul.
I cast away this cloak of gray that no longer serves its role.

I open arms, and eyes, and heart to welcome all that's new;
to say good-bye to what was mine, with no regret to rue.

For though a loss does leave a mark, it only marks the spot,
where new intentions will take root and dreams will fully sprout.

When ready to let go to make room for new growth, hold the paper to your heart and acknowledge what it contributed to your life, but say good-bye. Fold the paper over, away from you to release the negativity, tear it into pieces, and place them in your cauldron, on a heatproof surface.

Light the paper and watch it burn. Feel the tension leave your body as you let go of what was causing you stress or grief. Feel the lightness of new opportunities fill you from head to toe. Let the paper burn fully, if you can (or use the water to douse it, if needed). Let the ashes cool and bury them (if you are able) or wash them down the drain with clean water.

Give thanks for what you've learned.

THE BEST OF LUCK

Skip the wearin' o' the green and grab something red—preferably a representation of the charmingly cheerful fly agaric mushroom (page 87). Red symbolizes life, vitality, good fortune, and luck in many cultures, so turn to this lucky charmer for a change of fate. And, all mushrooms that have sprouted from the tiniest of spores in the harshest of conditions carry within them the energy of luck and survival. If you're in need of a lucky break, don't sit back and wait for it to come to you. Go find it, for it can be fleeting. You just need that one lucky glimpse of any lucky mushroom, and sometimes, all you have to do is change your outlook to change your luck.

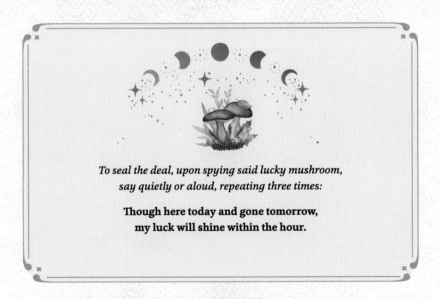

To seal the deal, upon spying said lucky mushroom,
say quietly or aloud, repeating three times:

Though here today and gone tomorrow,
my luck will shine within the hour.

FREE TO BE

Life's too short not to show up every day as your authentic, joyful self. If you find you need a little support in speaking your truth or telling your story, look to mushrooms for inspiration. There is no greater example of diversity: shape, size, color, texture, aroma, personality, habitat, taste, and more. One unique source of these manifestation energies is werewere-kōkako (page 113). This mushroom sings of the freedom to be you, uniquely you, and the courage to stand out in a crowd. The color blue corresponds with the throat chakra and lets communication flow freely, so choose anything blue as a stand-in, as needed.

When ready to let your uniqueness fly,
say quietly or aloud:

Hey, look at me and watch me shine, for life is grand and this is mine!

I'm not afraid to let you see the light within that I've set free.

It's truth I choose, for that, you see, will be my lasting legacy.

SPORES OF HOPE

Every mushroom can contain millions of spores, each imbued with the hope to grow and thrive. When times are tough or others around us, or in the interconnected humanity at large, are hurting, this simple ritual of creating a spore print can help send hopeful energies into the world to change the vibrations.

* Obtain a fresh mushroom; those with gills are best.
  NOTE: Beware of anything with white gills as it can often be poisonous; something from the grocery store is just fine.

* Carefully remove the stem. If needed, use a paring knife to carefully trim away the edge of the cap where it covers the gills to expose them all and fully.

* Place the cap, gill-side down, on a piece of light-colored paper, or a sheet of clear plastic, and cover the cap with a plastic or glass bowl or cup. Let the mushroom sit for 24 hours so that it can release its spores.

When ready to send your hopeful heartfelt wishes
into the world, say quietly or aloud:

O, beacon of light that burns within, ignite the spark of hope's delight.

For as it spreads from me to you, that hope within encourages still

the will to blossom bold and bright and carry forth hope's shining light.

* Carefully remove the cover you placed over the cap and lift the cap off the paper. If you used a piece of clear plastic, gently slip a piece of white (if the spores are dark) or dark-colored paper (if the spores are light) underneath to reveal the pattern.

* If you'd like to preserve the print, spray it with an artist's fixative, or try a light mist of hairspray. Or, take a photo and start an album of prints.

Take a moment to imagine those thousands of spores as individual people around the world connected by hope and their potential to grow and thrive. Close your eyes for a moment and see hope, as a light from your heart, brightening dark corners everywhere. Feel the joy that hope can bring.

BANISHING BAD

From the deadly death cap (page 91) to the stinky stinkhorn (page 151) and the luminous jack-o'-lantern (page 147), mushrooms have many natural ways to repel evil and its threat—from poison to taste to odor and shape to eerily warning light, each honed specifically to keep it safe from harm and help it thrive. With a mantra of "do no harm," you can still harness mushrooms' protective energies to cast away anything keeping you from realizing your goals and banish negativity from your life.

*Spend a moment in quiet meditation to set your
intentions, then say quietly or aloud:*

When evil lurks and spreads its fear, I cast this spell for all that's dear:

**Though some say no, or block the way,
succeed I will—you'll not hold sway.**

Thus, thrice proclaimed for all to hear, be banished now and disappear.

ABUNDANCE

Things are said to "mushroom quickly" for a reason: Mushrooms, such as the oyster (page 155) and fairy inkcap (page 105), do emerge seemingly full grown and in copious quantities, birthing millions of spores and miles of mycelia, spreading quickly and bringing with them an energy of fertility and abundance. And although an abundant life can mean many things to each of us—friends, love, money, opportunity—remember that whatever abundance you seek comes to you as you need it. Be patient.

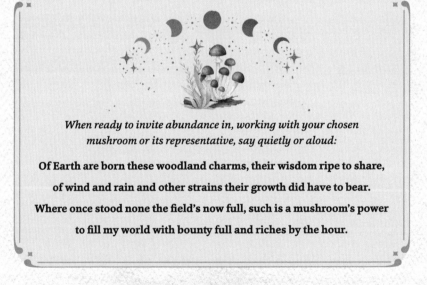

When ready to invite abundance in, working with your chosen mushroom or its representative, say quietly or aloud:

Of Earth are born these woodland charms, their wisdom ripe to share,

of wind and rain and other strains their growth did have to bear.

Where once stood none the field's now full, such is a mushroom's power

to fill my world with bounty full and riches by the hour.

PERSONAL GROWTH

To bloom where you land is a magical thing and, just like the millions of spores released by mushrooms to initiate new growth, where you land is not always where you choose. Landing outside of our comfort zone is always scary but ripe for new growth. So, learning to adapt and bloom under many conditions can ensure that growth and renewal you seek. Magic mushrooms, or *Psilocybe*, are known to grow all over the world, in widely diverse climates and habitats, providing they receive enough rain, and we can take great example from them—figuratively, of course. A little meditation (see page 59), like raindrops, to prepare our hearts to nurture our intentions, can be helpful, too.

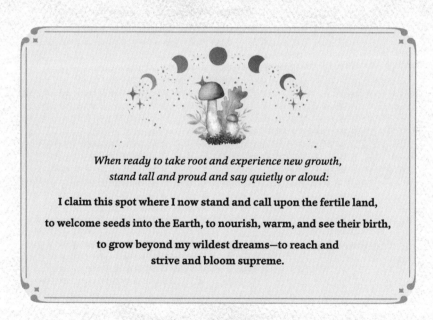

When ready to take root and experience new growth,
stand tall and proud and say quietly or aloud:

I claim this spot where I now stand and call upon the fertile land,

to welcome seeds into the Earth, to nourish, warm, and see their birth,

to grow beyond my wildest dreams—to reach and
strive and bloom supreme.

AGING GRACEFULLY

The mushroom in many cultures has been a long-believed source of immortality. And, it seems, research has uncovered a scientific reason to continue the belief in this magic. Mushrooms, in general, are known to contain high levels of antioxidants—and two specifically, ergothioneine and glutathione—that may help fight aging and maintain health. The top-ranked examples include the reishi, for immortality; porcini, for its quantity of antioxidants; lion's mane, for health and longevity; and Cordyceps, for energy.

Whether you choose skin care, supplements, or diet as the way to harness the energy, why not boost the antiaging magic a bit with your own innate magic?

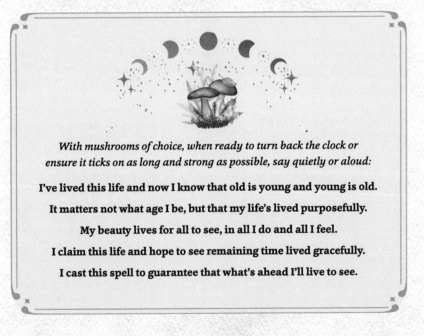

With mushrooms of choice, when ready to turn back the clock or ensure it ticks on as long and strong as possible, say quietly or aloud:

I've lived this life and now I know that old is young and young is old.

It matters not what age I be, but that my life's lived purposefully.

My beauty lives for all to see, in all I do and all I feel.

I claim this life and hope to see remaining time lived gracefully.

I cast this spell to guarantee that what's ahead I'll live to see.

THE "MOREL" OF THE
STORY—SHARE THE WEALTH

Among the most prized and expensive of mushrooms, the magnificent morel mushroom (page 141) is called the chef's mushroom. With edible (and 100 percent positively identified) mushrooms at the core of so many culinary traditions, let the magic of meals conjured with them spread love and sustenance to those you hold dear. Invite others to join you around the table, or take meals to those unable to leave their homes. When we can share our good fortune (no matter the wealth), seasoned with intention, our bounty grows threefold.

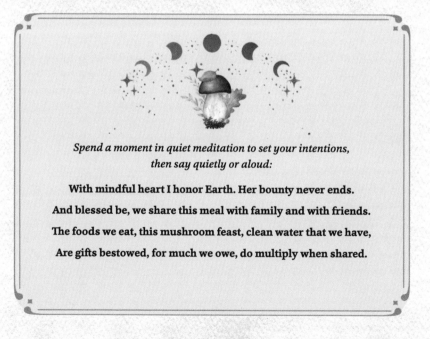

Spend a moment in quiet meditation to set your intentions,
then say quietly or aloud:

With mindful heart I honor Earth. Her bounty never ends.

And blessed be, we share this meal with family and with friends.

The foods we eat, this mushroom feast, clean water that we have,

Are gifts bestowed, for much we owe, do multiply when shared.

FAIRY RING OFFERING

The infamous fairy ring—not everyone believes it's something to be avoided! It is a source, too, of good luck and fairy blessings. Once spied, do not disturb the ring. The circle represents a connection to the circles found everywhere in Nature and marks a sacred space full of positive, protective energy, derived from the circle itself and the mushrooms that have formed it as well as those Good People who dwell within the circle. If found at dusk, listen for the sounds of music and laughter emanating from the fairy celebration typically held within the ring. Entering the ring often means being transported to the mystical fairy kingdom where magic and adventure await. However, a simple offering left for the fairies, who adore gifts, and for Mother Nature, who gave birth to the ring, can be an invitation for their blessings in your life and a symbol of gratitude for Nature's bounty.

Offerings should be made with care, as well as represent a part of you, and offerings should always be made from a generous heart. **NOTE:** If you leave offerings anywhere other than on your own property, always ask permission from the property owner or other authority, if need be, and leave only natural offerings that are sure to do no harm to any plant or animal life (including humans) that may come upon them. If leaving offerings on your property, again, please do so safely and with the knowledge that what you leave will do no harm. And, plan on cleaning up anything the fae leave behind to prepare the space for your next offering.

Here are some suggestions to help you plan your offering.

* **BIRDSEED:** A double offering—the birds will be grateful, too, and you'll doubly impress the fairies by taking care of the birds.
* **CLEAN WATER:** In a larger container for sharing or in acorn caps for bathing or sipping (before the bath, obviously!).
* **DRIED HERBS AND FLOWERS:** In months when summer has passed.
* **FALLEN LEAVES:** Write a message to the Universe on fallen leaves and let it drift on the wind to be heard.

* **FLOWER SEEDS:** For the fairies to plant in their gardens.
* **FRESH, ORGANIC BERRIES:** Preferably from your garden, but you can purchase them, left on a small cloth set up for a fairy picnic!
* **HONEY:** Another fairy favorite—maybe even the most favorite!
* **MUSIC:** Think wind chimes, or sing or play an instrument.
* **NATURE'S FOUND THINGS:** Collections of seashells, twigs, stones, pine cones, nuts, flower heads, or flower petals.
* **WORDS AND LAUGHTER:** Speak from your heart or use the words provided here.

When your offering is ready, take a moment to thank the Universe for its gifts given so freely. Establish an open mind and an open heart to receive the fairies' response.

Place your offering, inside or outside the fairy ring,
and say quietly or aloud:

This fairy ring lives as the circle of life, which I honor
and tend with these gifts to delight.

I call on the spirits, the wind, Earth, and rain,
the rays of the Sun, and Moon Goddess by name.

This circle is blessed and its treasure is rare—each soul
that does seek it has nothing to fear.

As I step in this circle and feel its embrace, my heart blooms
with wonder for Nature's sweet face.

Conclusion

T HE HUMBLE MUSHROOM is not so humble once you look beneath the surface, and the revelations found there are practical as well as inspirational, not to mention magical. Hidden within the mystical mushroom could be the keys to cures for everyday ailments and serious illness, as well as the blueprints for managing life on Earth in a way that sustains her life, too. And our modern quest to regain the ancient connection to Earth and the plants she produces is a natural way to explore the bountiful treasure that is mushrooms.

In a seemingly endless array of forms and unfathomable number of species, the opportunities for discoveries yet to be made can seem mind blowing. Something that presents from Nature in such stunning variety must surely be Nature's way of teaching us not to take anything for granted, and to be curious enough to uncover her secrets in order to improve her future as well as ours. And as fungi are believed to have led the way for plants and animals to exist on Earth, why wouldn't they also be a way to nourish, heal, protect, and evolve those plants and animals?

So, take up the cause in whatever way mushrooms speak to you. Engage, explore, encourage, and sow the spores of growth. Support others in their journey. Beautify and enrich the world with your talents and abilities. Be the light when needed and the unseen source of strength to lift up those around you. Root out the bad and nourish the good. Embrace the darkness as a time to renew. Offer a healing touch or a dose of reality. Turn on the charm and turn up the fun. Invite others to dance in your fairy ring. Grow where you land and thrive where you grow.

Whatever the questions, mushrooms may just hold the answers. Take a moment to listen—and be grateful for and honor Nature's truly magical and mysterious ways.

Acknowledgments

ALTHOUGH IT FEELS LIKE it at times, creating a book is not a solitary endeavor. Thank you to all who helped bring this book to life. You are the roots that keep it strong and help it grow.

To Quarto publisher Rage Kindelsperger, my immense and heartfelt thanks for tilling the fertile soil from which these words do sprout and nurturing their growth with faith and expert guidance.

To Elizabeth You, for careful pruning and harvesting to ensure the manuscript grew into its best self.

To all the teams at Quarto, for their dedication to supporting authors and their incredible talents that bring beautiful books into the world.

To Westerville Public Library, for its outstanding contribution to community and its invaluable service to this author.

To Nature, for her bounty and inspiration.

To all my friends and family who cast magic into my life daily, thank you for your love and support.

To John, for roots that support growth and change and love that transforms all.

Finally, the world would be such a dull place without the magic of books. It is a magic multiplied exponentially each time a reader opens one and brings their own magic to it.

References

Allied Market Research. "Functional Mushroom Market." October 2021. Accessed 6/20/2022. https://www.alliedmarketresearch.com/functional-mushroom -market-A14273.

Anderson, James B., Johann N. Bruhn, Dahlia Kasimer, Hao Wang, Nicolas Rodrigue, and Myron L. Smith. "Clonal Evolution and Genome Stability in a 2,500-Year-Old Fungal Individual." *bioRxiv* 377234. doi:https://doi.org/10.1101/377234.

Arora, David. *Mushrooms Demystified: A Comprehensive Guide to the Fleshy Fungi.* 2nd ed. Berkeley, CA: Ten Speed Press, 1986.

Atlas of Living Australia: ala.org.au.

Barrett, Frederick S., Katrin H. Preller, and Mendel Kaelen. "Psychedelics and Music: Neuroscience and Therapeutic Implications." *International Review of Psychiatry* 30, no. 4 (2018): 350–362. doi:10.1080/09540261.2018.1484342.

Bertelsen, Cynthia D. *Mushroom: A Global History.* London: Reaktion Books Ltd., 2013.

Bone, Eugenia. *Mycophilia.* Emmaus, PA: Rodale, 2011.

British Mycological Society. "Pioneering Scientist or Passionate Amateur." British Mycological Society. June 20, 2017. https://www.britmycolsoc.org.uk/education /news/beatr.

Brooks, Rebecca Beatrice. "History of the Salem Witch Trials." August 18, 2011. Accessed June 4, 2022. https://historyofmassachusetts.org/the-salem-witch-trials.

Brooks, Rebecca Beatrice. "What Caused the Salem Witch Trials?" History of Massachusetts.org. June 30, 2018. Accessed June 4, 2022. https://historyofmassachusetts. org/salem-witch-trials-causes.

Burk, William R. "Puffball Usages Among North American Indians." *Journal of Ethnobiology* 3, no. 1 (May 1983): 55–62.

Campbell Soup Company. "10 Things You Didn't Know about Green Bean Casserole." Campbell History. November 17, 2020. Accessed June 12, 2022. https://www.campbellsoupcompany.com/newsroom/campbell-history/10-things -you-didnt-know-about-green-bean-casserole.

Capasso, L. "5300 Years Ago, the Ice Man Used Natural Laxatives and Antibiotics." *Lancet* 352, no. 9143 (1998): 1864. doi:10.1016/S0140-6736(05)79939-6. PMID 9851424. S2CID 40027370.

Caporael, Linnda R. "Ergotism: The Satan Loosed in Salem?: Convulsive Ergotism May Have Been a Physiological Basis for the Salem Witchcraft Crisis in 1692." *Science* 192, no. 4234 (April 2, 1976): 21–26. doi:10.1126/science.769159.

Casselman, Anne. "Strange but True: The Largest Organism on Earth Is a Fungus." *Scientific American*. October 4, 2007. Accessed April 9, 2022. https://www. scientificamerican.com/article/strange-but-true-largest-organism-is-fungus.

Cornell Mushroom Blog. Cornell University. https://blog.mycology.cornell.edu.

Daley, Beth. "Liberty Cap: The Surprising Tale of How Europe's Magic Mushroom Got Its Name." *The Conversation*. November 27, 2020. https://theconversation.com/liberty -cap-the-surprising-tale-of-how-europes-magic-mushroom-got-its-name-130668.

Dressaire, Emilie, Lisa Yamada, Boya Song, and Marcus Roper. "Mushrooms Use Convectively Created Airflows to Disperse Their Spores." *Proceedings of the National Academy of Sciences of the United States of America* 113, no. 11 (February 29, 2016): 2833–2838. https://doi.org/10.1073/pnas.1509612113.

Dugan, Frank M. "Baba Yaga and the Mushrooms." *Fungi* 10, no. 2 (Summer 2017): 6–18.

Dugan, Frank M. *Conspectus of World Ethnomycology: Fungi in Ceremonies, Crafts, Diets, Medicines, and Myths*. St. Paul, MN: American Phytopathological Society, 2011.

Dugan, Frank M. "Fungi, Folkways, and Fairy Tales: Mushrooms & Mildews in Stories, Remedies, and Rituals from Oberon to the Internet." *North American Fungi* 3, no. 7 (August 29, 2008): 23–72. doi:10.2509/naf2008.003.0074.

Dugan, Frank M. *Hidden Histories and Ancient Mysteries of Witches, Plants, and Fungi*. St. Paul, MN: American Phytopathological Society, 2015.

Encyclopaedia Britannica: Britannica.com.

Fearnley, Kirstin. "Weird & Wonderful Creatures: Bleeding Tooth Fungus." American Association for the Advance of Science: News. July 5, 2016. Accessed March 23, 2022. https://aaas.org/news/weird-wonderful-creatures-bleeding-tooth-fungus.

Ferguson, Yuna L., and Kennon M. Sheldon. "Trying to Be Happier Really Can Work: Two Experimental Studies." *The Journal of Positive Psychology* 8, no. 1 (2013): 23–33. https://doi.org/10.1080/17439760.2012.747000.

Findlay, W. P. K. *Fungi: Folklore, Fiction, and Fact*. Eureka, CA: Mad River Press, 1982.

Geddes, Linda. "Europe's First Psychedelic Drug Trial Firm to Open in London." *The Guardian*. May 9, 2022. Accessed July 1, 2022. https://www.theguardian.com/ science/2022/may/09/europes-first-psychedelic-drug-trial-firm-to-open-in-london.

Grieve, M. *A Modern Herbal in Two Volumes: Vol. I A–H*. New York: Dover Publications, Inc., 1971.

Hálek, Václav. *Hudební Atlas Hub (The Musical Atlas of Mushrooms)*. Internet Archive.

Harding, Patrick. *Mushroom Miscellany*. London: Collins (an imprint of HarperCollins), 2008.

Hassett, Maribeth O., Mark W. F. Fischer, and Nicholas P. Money. "Mushrooms as Rainmakers: How Spores Act as Nuclei for Raindrops." *PLOS One* (October 28, 2015): https://doi.org/10.1371/journal.pone.014040.7.

Herbst, Sharon Tyler, and Ron Herbst. *The New Food Lover's Companion*, 5th ed. Highland Ranch, CO: Peterson's Publishing LLC, 2013.

Heuschkel, Kristin, and Kim P. C. Kuypers. "Depression, Mindfulness, and Psilocybin: Possible Complementary Effects of Mindfulness Meditation and Psilocybin in the Treatment of Depression. A Review." *Frontiers in Psychiatry* (March 31, 2020). https://doi.org/10.3389/fpsyt.2020.00224.

Hill, Rowena. "Meeting the Firestarting Fungus." Royal Botanic Gardens, Kew. August 8, 2019. Accessed June 3, 2022. https://www.kew.org/read-and-watch /king-alfreds-cakes-fungus.

History.com Editors. "History of Witches." *History.com*. September 12, 2017; updated October 20, 2020. Accessed June 3, 2022. https://www.history.com/topics/folklore /history-of-witches.

Hong, Lei, Ma Zun, and Wu Wutong. "Anti-Diabetic Effect of Alpha-Glucan from Fruit Body of Maitake (*Grifola frondosa*) on KK-Ay Mice." *The Journal of Pharmacy and Pharmacology* 59, no. 4 (April 2007): 575–82. doi:10.1211/jpp.59.4.0013.

International Union for Conservation of Nature. The Global Fungal Red List Initiative. http://iucn.ekoo.se/en/iucn/welcome.

Joshi, Sudeep, Ellexis Cook, and Manu S. Mannoor. "Bacterial Nanobionics via 3D Printing." *Nano Letters* 18, no. 12 (2018): 7448–7456. https://doi.org/10.1021/ acs.nanolett.8b02642.

Kalaras, Michael D., John P. Richie, Ana Calcagnotto, and Robert B. Beelman. "Mushrooms: A Rich Source of the Antioxidants Ergothioneine and Glutathione." *Food Chemistry* 233 (October 15, 2017): 429–433. https://doi.org/10.1016/ j.foodchem.2017.04.109.

Kirk, P. M., P. F. Cannon, D. W. Minter, and J. A. Stalpers. *Ainsworth & Bisby's Dictionary of the Fungi*, 10th ed. Wallingford, Oxon, UK: CAB International, 2008.

Kubo, K., H. Aoki, and H. Nanba. "Anti-Diabetic Activity Present in the Fruit Body of *Grifola frondosa* (Maitake). I." *Biological & Pharmaceutical Bulletin* 17, no. 8 (August 1994): 1106–10. doi:10.1248/bpb.17.1106.

Letcher, Andy. *Shroom: A Cultural History of the Magic Mushroom*. New York: Ecco, 2007.

Li, Tinggang, Chen Zhang, Kun-Lin Yang, and Jianzhong He. "Unique Genetic Cassettes in a Thermoanaerobacterium Contribute to Simultaneous Conversion of Cellulose and Monosugars into Butanol." *Science Advances* 4, no. 3 (2018): e1701475. doi:10.1126/sciadv.1701475.

Lincoff, Gray. *The Complete Mushroom Hunter: An Illustrated Guide to Foraging, Harvesting, and Enjoying Wild Mushrooms*, rev. ed. Beverly, MA: Quarto Publishing Group, 2017, 2010.

Lloyd, Ellen. "Mysterious Ancient Mushrooms in Myths and Legends: Sacred, Feared, and Worshiped Among Ancient Civilizations." *Ancient Pages*. September 14, 2016. https://ancientpages.com/2016/09/14/mysterious-ancient-mushrooms-in-myths-and-legends-sacred-feared-and-worshiped-among-ancient-civilizations-2.

Lonik, Larry. *The Curious Morel*, 4th ed. Mechanicsburg, PA: Stackpole Books, 2012.

Ma, B.-J., et al. "Hericenones and Erinacines: Stimulators of Nerve Growth Factor (NGF) Biosynthesis in *Hericium erinaceus*." *Mycology* 1 (2010).

MacReady, Norra. "Opening Doors of Perception: Psychedelic Drugs and End-of-Life Care." *Journal of the National Cancer Institute* 104, no. 21 (November 7, 2012): 1619–1620. https://doi.org/10.1093/jnci/djs468.

Margolin, Madison, and Shelby Hartman. "Inside 9/20, the Holiday for Psychedelic Mushrooms." *Rolling Stone*. September 18, 2020. https://www.rollingstone.com/culture/culture-features/9-20-psychedelic-mushroom-holiday-psilocybin-1061753.

Market Data Forecast. "Edible Mushroom Market." January 2022. https://marketdataforecast.com/market-reports/edible-mushroom-market.

Marley, Greg A. *Chanterelle Dreams, Amanita Nightmares*. White River Junction, VT: Chelsea Green Publishing, 2010.

Martinez, Marisol. "Johns Hopkins Receives First Federal Grant for Psychedelic Treatment Research in 50 Years." Johns Hopkins University. HUB. October 20, 2021. Accessed March 18, 2022. https://hub.jhu.edu/2021/10/20/first-nih-grant-for-psychedelics-in-50-years.

Martino, Victor. "Mushroom Mania—The Vegetable's Rise in Packaged Food." *JUSTFood*. November 2, 2021. Updated February 1, 2022. https://www.just-food.com/analysis/mushroom-mania-the-vegetables-rise-in-packaged-food.

Miles P. G., and S. T. Chang. *Mushrooms: Cultivation, Nutritional Value, Medicinal Effect, and Environmental Impact*. Boca Raton, FL: CRC Press, 2004.

Millman, Lawrence. *Fungipedia: A Brief Compendium of Mushroom Lore*. Princeton, NJ, and Oxford, UK: Princeton University Press, 2019.

Money, Nicholas P. "Hyphal and Mycelial Consciousness: The Concept of the Fungal Mind." *Fungal Biology* 125, no. 4 (April 2021): 257–346. https://doi.org/10.1016 /j.funbio.2021.02.001.

Money, Nicholas P. *Mushrooms: A Natural and Cultural History*. London: Reaktion Books Ltd., 2017.

Money, Nicholas P. "The Fungal Mind: On the Evidence for Mushroom Intelligence." *Psyche*. Accessed March 4, 2022. https://psyche.co/ideas/the-fungal-mind -on-the-evidence-for-mushroom-intelligence.

Morgan, Adrian. *Toads and Toadstools: The Natural History, Folklore, and Cultural Oddities of a Strange Association*. Berkeley, CA: Celestial Arts, 1995.

Mushroom Hour Podcast. "Feral Fungi—Alchemycology, Astromycology & Spagyric Tinctures." Episode 115, featuring Jason Scott. *Mushroom Hour*. March 16, 2022. https://www.welcometomushroomhour.com/blogs/podcasts/ep-115-feral-fungi-alchemycology-astromycology-spagyric-tinctures-feat-jason-scott.

National Institutes of Health. "Classics of Traditional Chinese Medicine: From the History of Medicine Division, National Library of Medicine." An Online Version of an Exhibit Held at the NLM, October 19, 1999–May 30, 2000. U. S. National Library of Medicine. Website last updated 2009. https://www.nlm.nih.gov/exhibition/ chinesemedicine/credits.html.

National Trust: https://www.nationaltrust.org.uk.

North American Mycological Association: https://namyco.org.

North American Mycological Association. Registry of Mushrooms in Works of Art: https://namyco.org/art_registry.php.

Oliveira, Anderson G., Cassius V. Stevani, Hans E. Waldenmaier, Vadim Viviani, Jillian M. Emerson, Jennifer J. Loros, and Jay C. Dunlap. "Circadian Control Sheds Light on Fungal Bioluminescence." *Current Biology* 25, no. 7 (March 30, 2015): 964–968. https://doi.org/10.1016/j.cub.2015.02.021.

Peintner, U., R. Pöder, and T. Pümpel. "The Iceman's Fungi." *Mycological Research* 102, no. 10 (1998): 1153–1162.

Pliny the Elder. *The Natural History*. "Chapter 46. Mushrooms: Peculiarities of Their Growth." Perseus Digital Library. http://data.perseus.org/citations/ urn:cts:latinLit:phi0978.phi001.perseus-eng1:22.46.

Pouliot, Alison. "The Glowing Ghost Mushroom Looks Like It Comes from a Fungal Netherworld." *The Conversation*. February 14, 2019. Accessed March 6, 2022. https://theconversation.com/the-glowing-ghost-mushroom-looks-like-it-comes-from-a-fungal-netherworld-111607.

Royal Botanic Gardens, London, Kew Gardens: https://kew.org.

Rubenstein, Jake. "Tiny but Deadly: Cigarette Butts Are the Most Commonly Polluted Plastic." EarthDay.org. August 28, 2020. Accessed June 18, 2022. https://www.earthday.org/tiny-but-deadly-cigarette-butts-are-the-most-commonly-polluted-plastic.

Sanford, James. H. "Japan's 'Laughing Mushrooms.'" *Economic Botany* 26, no. 2 (April–June 1972): 174–181. http://www.jstor.org/stable/4253336.

Schmitt, Craig L., and Michael L. Tatum. "The Malheur National Forest: Location of the World's Largest Living Organism (The Humongous Fungus)." United States Department of Agriculture. 2008. https://www.fs.usda.gov/Internet/FSE_DOCUMENTS/fsbdev3_033146.pdf.

Schwartzenberg, Louie, director, and Mark Monroe, writer. *Fantastic Fungi*. Moving Art, 2019.

Shakespeare, William. *The Tempest*. London: Blount and Jaggard, 1623.

Shao, Ling-Xiao, Clara Liao, Ian Gregg, Neil K. Savalia, and Kristina Delagarza. "Psilocybin Induces Rapid and Persistent Growth of Dendritic Spines in Frontal Cortex *In Vivo*." *Neuron* 109, no. 16 (July 5, 2021): 2535–2544. doi:https://doi.org/10.1016/j.neuron.2021.06.008.

Sharvit, Lital, Rinat Bar-Shalom, Naiel Azzam, Yaniv Yechiel, Solomon Wasser, and Fuad Fares. "*Cyathus striatus* Extract Induces Apoptosis in Human Pancreatic Cancer Cells and Inhibits Xenograft Tumor Growth In Vivo." *Cancers* (Basel) 13, no. 9 (May 2021): 2017. doi:10.3390/cancers13092017.

Sheldrake, Merlin. *Entangled Life: How Fungi Make Our Worlds, Change Our Minds & Shape Our Futures*. New York: Random House, 2020.

Shroder, Tom. "'Apparently Useless': The Accidental Discovery of LSD." *The Atlantic*. September 9, 2014. Accessed October 26, 2022. https://www.theatlantic.com/health/archive/2014/09/the-accidental-discovery-of-lsd/379564.

Smith, M., J. Bruhn, and J. Anderson. "The Fungus *Armillaria bulbosa* Is Among the Largest and Oldest Living Organisms." *Nature* 356 (1992): 428–431.

Spooner, Brian, and Thomas Læssøe. "The Folklore of 'Gasteromycetes.'" *Mycologist* 8 part 3 (August 1994): 119–123.

Tavares, Frank (ed.). "Could Future Homes on the Moon and Mars Be Made of Fungi?" NASA-Ames Research Center. NASA.gov. January 14, 2020. www.nasa.gov/feature/ames/myco-architecture.

The Beatrix Potter Society: https://beatrixpottersociety.org.uk.

The Buddhist Centre: https://thebuddhistcentre.com.

The Linnean Society of London: https://linnean.org.

The Mushroom Council: https://mushroomcouncil.com.

The Wildlife Trusts: https://wildlifetrusts.org.

Toussaint-Samat, Maguelonne. *A History of Food*. Chichester, UK: Wiley-Blackwell, 2009.

Turner, Nancy, and Alain Cuerrier. "'Frog's Umbrella' and 'Ghost's Face Powder': The Cultural Roles of Mushrooms and Other Fungi for Canadian Indigenous Peoples." *Botany* 100 (2022): 183–205. dx.doi.org/10.1139/cjb-2021-0052.

United States Department of Agriculture: https://USDA.gov.

United States Forest Service. "The Mighty Fungi." United States Department of Agriculture. Accessed June 3, 2022. https://www.fs.usda.gov/wildflowers/ethnobotany/Mind_and_Spirit/fungi.shtml.

University of Auckland, New Zealand, Metabolomics Lab. https://metabolomics.blogs.auckland.ac.nz/2017/03/21/research-areas.

Volk, Tom. Tom Volk's Fungi. "Fungus of the Month." Department of Biology. University of Wisconsin-La Crosse. https://botit.botany.wisc.edu/toms_fungi.

Wasson, Gordon R. *The Wondrous Mushroom: Mycolatry in Mesoamerica*. New York: McGraw-Hill Book Company, 1980.

Wilson, N., J. Hollinger, et al. *Mushroom Observer*. https://mushroomobserver.org.

Woodland Trust: https://www.woodlandtrust.org.uk.

World Health Organization. "Depression." September 13, 2021. Accessed June 24, 2022. https://www.who.int/en/news-room/fact-sheets/detail/depression.

Xiong, S., C. Martín, L. Eilertsen, M. Wei, O. Myronycheva, S. H. Larsson, et al. "Energy-Efficient Substrate Pasteurisation for Combined Production of Shiitake Mushroom (*Lentinula edodes*) and Bioethanol." *Bioresource Technology* 274 (February 2019): 65–72. doi:10.1016/j.biortech.2018.11.071.

Yu, Zhenzhong, and Reinhard Fischer. "Light Sensing and Responses in Fungi." *Nature Reviews Microbiology* 17 (2019): 25–36. doi:https://doi.org/10.1038/s41579-018-0109-x.

Index